Mandala
The Art of
Creating
Future

Mandala
The Art of
Creating
Future

June-Elleni Laine

BOOKS

Winchester, UK
Washington, USA

First published by O-Books, 2009
O-Books is an imprint of John Hunt Publishing Ltd., Laurel House, Station Approach,
Alresford, Hants, SO24 9JH, UK
office1@o-books.net
www.o-books.com

For distributor details and how to order please visit the 'Ordering' section on our website.

Text copyright: June-Elleni Laine 2008

ISBN: 978 1 84694 194 8

A CIP catalogue record for this book is available from the British Library.

Design: Stuart Davies

Printed in the UK by CPI Antony Rowe
Printed in the USA by Offset Paperback Mfrs, Inc

We operate a distinctive and ethical publishing philosophy in all
areas of our business, from our global network of authors to
production and worldwide distribution.

CONTENTS

Mandala

The Art Of Creating Future

My heart felt thanks to teachers, students and friends…
You know who you are, we are all one!
J-E

☺

Preface

All social animals communicate with each other, from the tiniest ant to the largest whale, but only humans have developed a language, which is more than a series of learnt sounds and signals. Our ability to communicate in this way is probably how we climbed to the top of the survival tree, the left-brain hemisphere bringing us the aptitude of logic, discernment, practicality and stability.

Art is as unique to us as a species as being able to talk. It has been in the human consciousness for more than 40,000 years. We have developed the ability to create art as a plan or aspect of the future and not just to copy what we see. Our ancestors Homo erectus left traces of art in caves over 40,000 years ago.

For an ability to have survived the test of time over tens of thousands of years, must make it an important skill, and even fundamental to our survival. The right-brain hemisphere's ability to tap into the Tao or Zeitgeist – the spirit of time and place – to be intuitive and flexible – is probably why we stayed at the top of the survival tree so far!

The large majority of us enjoy creating art when we are children, but by the age of around nine most of us stop. We either decide for ourselves that we cannot draw, or else we are told that we cannot!

This book brings forward reasons why art (a divine feminine principle) is now, at this particular time in our evolution, more important than ever. Why we need to revive it as a common tool to create our future or otherwise walk in the shoes of Neanderthal, who went extinct!

Introduction

*"Prayer is not an old woman's idle amusement. Properly understood
and applied, it is the most potent instrument of action."*
~ ***Gandhi***

Are we at last beginning to realise that our intentions, prayers
and thoughts can actually affect physical reality? Different
strands of [1]science and the media are exploring ideas that could
change how many of us view life, the universe and everything.
Instead of regarding prayer as wishful thinking, we may now
start to believe that our ability to affect physical reality is directly
related to our ability to focus our attention and connect. These are
exciting times to be alive!

The burning question still remains, how can we focus and
connect for long enough to manifest our intent and in any case,
how long is long enough?

Traditional spiritual leaders have indicated that hours of
repetitive prayer, chanting or meditation are necessary to focus
the mind and quieten the ego. Neurology is also leaning this way,
as the Dalai Lama has joined forces with US scientists encour-
aging cutting edge brain monitoring experiments on Tibetan
monks and Lamas while they meditate. Their brains show significant changes as they focus on compassion. But let's face it, when
we get right down to it, most of us are challenged to focus even
for short periods of time – apparently we lose focus six to eight
times every minute in our daily life – annoying isn't it?

It's no wonder we are left feeling frustrated and as if we cannot
affect change in our lives. We may also be tempted to agree that
only adept yogis or meditators can hold their attention for long
enough to manifest anything, so we give up even before making
a start.

The good news is, there is something we can all learn that will help us create what we intend. There is evidence to suggest that we have an innate ability for it, but because it stems so far back along the time-line, many of us have forgotten its true value.

I am referring to the Mandala. It has been used throughout the world for personal growth, self-expression, and spiritual transformation for thousands – probably tens of thousands – of years.

There is evidence of Mandalas in cave paintings and for its regular use in shamanic practice, as well as its later development in early Asian civilizations, who regarded the Mandala as a model of the world, or the universe.

The word Mandala is derived from the root *manda*, meaning *essence*, and *la*, meaning *container*; thus a Mandala is a container of essence.

It took until the 20th Century for the West to consciously rediscover the role of the Mandala. Carl Jung believed creating Mandalas helped to make the unconscious conscious. Joseph Campbell describes drawing them as bringing the scattered aspects of your life together, finding a centre, leading us to wholeness. More recently Richard Moss (among others) uses Mandalas as a system for personal growth, reconciling the mental and emotional reality within us and the reality 'out there'.

In this book we go further; we go to the root of matter. Recent years have seen an explosion of interest in the quantum fields of energy in which we exist, and that connect all things together.

It's not the place here to go into this extensively, (see Appendix 1 for further reading) but various scientists and parapsychologists are suggesting that we can indeed 'sense' beyond the normal five senses, as we tap into these energy fields. During this interaction we can and we do discover abilities that are way beyond what we would logically expect. Maybe this is because our interface with the creative energy fields is located in the non-verbal part of the brain, which communicates in flavours and impressions, rather than in logical words. This is the part of the mind where we are not limited by what we think we already 'know', and we are free to explore many other possibilities.

So in discovering how to successfully interact with these energy fields, increase our multi-sensory awareness, find our centre and restore our balance with creation, art is so much more important than logic and ego. And of all art, the Mandala is the most sacred. It brings our intuition and logic, our right and left-brain hemispheres, into balance. This cooperative practice is what I believe activates the very blueprint of creation (way down in the root of the quantum field).

This 'spiritual' or 'shamanic' ritual elevates mankind from the realms of passive animalist observer, to that of active Co-Creator.

The Mandala therefore is truly the container of essence, the Holy Grail for which we have been searching, a mystical vessel holding miraculous powers, lost for centuries but right here under our very noses!

So let us now explore our relationship with the Mandala, drawing on the experiences of friends, colleagues, students and clients that have inspired this book. Let's explore how it can simply and powerfully carry the essence of our intentions forwards into manifestation. We wouldn't dream of building a house without first using art to draw out the plans. In the same way, art in the form of a Mandala can be used to draw out our intentions and bring them to life!

Chapter 1

What Is A Mandala Really?

"... I knew that in finding the Mandala as an expression of the self I had attained what was for me the ultimate."
~ C. G. Jung

Mandala is a Sanskrit word, meaning circle, round, totality, completion or even primordial sound. However, let's not be limited by the idea of a circle; even in my brief experience of transliteration from Sanskrit to English, I have realised that so much can be lost or misunderstood when a word is translated into English.

It reminds me of trying to interpret inspiration into logic. That said, as we delve a little deeper, the word Mandala is derived from the root *Manda*, which means *essence*, energy or spirit, and by adding the suffix *la* to any Sanskrit word, it becomes the container or vessel for it; thus revealing the *Mandala* as a *container for essence, energy or spirit.*

This also seems to describe you and me perfectly... doesn't it? Could it be that We are the Ultimate Mandala?

I'll discuss this again in Chapter 8, but first let's explore Art as the container of energy.

The word Mandala is familiar today as a synonym for 'sacred space' throughout the world, and this definition is included in English dictionaries and encyclopaedias. They define Mandala as a pictorial geometric design intended to symbolize the entire universe.

Although mostly associated with religion and spirituality in many parts of the Asia and the Far East, Mandalas are also found in Aboriginal sand paintings, within Hindu cosmology, amongst the ruins of ancient Mayan architecture, as part of Celtic, Roman, Grecian, Egyptian as well as Iranian, Persian and Russian artefacts. They also appear to form potent symbols made by tribal nations such as the Native American Indians, Polynesians, Africans, and Maoris.

Mandalas feature in most shamanistic and ritual-based traditions as cave paintings, masks, shields, amulets, charms and talisman as well as body and facial painting or tattooing. These are all powerful forms of non-verbal communication directed at the subconscious and unconscious mind as well as the conscious.

This non-verbal communication has been generally undervalued in the west, mostly used between mothers and children until they learn to speak. After we have acquired the dominant language of our culture, our non-verbal knowing is gradually pushed down into the sub-consciousness, where it becomes a sleeping partner.

So it remains on the fringe, coming to light mostly through mediums and psychics, hypnosis, art therapy and more recently [2]NLP. It naturally tries to move back into consciousness at times when we are stressed and cannot cope with life in our 'normal' way of being, when it can appear as intuition, as the memory of a dream, or as strange and even frightening experiences, but it isn't given any mainstream importance. "Don't worry, it's just your imagination, or it's only a dream," we are told. We are encouraged to ignore it and at best to go and see a doctor, psychologist or psychiatrist where we can talk about it or take drugs to suppress it again.

Historically in past cultures and even still in some tribal cultures of today, dreams are very significant to the whole community, no matter who dreams them. Even a child's dreams are given credence.

Modern day anthropologists, such as [3]Marianne George, who

lived and worked amongst the Barok tribe in Papua New Guinea, reportedly experienced the amazing capacity of dreams first hand, when a tribal elder actually visited her in a dream one night. The following day the elder's two sons paid Marianne an unexpected and illuminating visit to ensure she had understood and remembered their mother's message from the night before. This encounter seems to be evidence indeed that dreams can be developed as conscious communication.

I am one of many people that can remember my dreams. Looking back, I know on a deep level that they are messages of guidance for me, even though I don't always understand them logically at the time. They take a little time to contemplate and digest. As a child and teenager, my most recurring dreams were of crossing bridges, bridges of many different types, and it's no surprise that bridges became very alluring to me. In fact they became such a focus that I eventually shared them with my schoolteacher during a careers lesson.

"I think I should design bridges," I announced, " I dream about them all the time."

To which he promptly advised me that civil engineering was the way to go. I accepted the left-brain subjects needed to study for this career path, but sometime along the way I starting feeling uninspired. I began to realise this literal interpretation was not as helpful as it could have been, which may have been realised sooner if my 'tribe' – like the Barok – had been more familiar with the value of messages in our dreams. Even so, synchronicity took a hand and delivered me into the creative world of fashion design were I was to find a window of opportunity using my ability to design while daydreaming across an inner dimensional bridge!

So it was that during my career as a designer I bridged dimensions while I was mindlessly sketching. I was used to daydreaming as I sketched; I had done it for as long as I could remember, so to me it was normal. I am not sure exactly when I realised it wasn't as 'normal' as I thought, and that it was in fact of great benefit to me. It is a way of tapping into a stream of otherworldly consciousness that has inspired my most successful ideas. Maybe it was because I could earn money using this ability at this time that my logical side gave it a chance. I can't say for sure, but eventually I overcame my initial anxieties – [4]including several frightening and unexplainable experiences – and focused on learning how to switch in and out of this strange state of awareness. To journey like a shaman into other dream-worlds and bring back messages. Since then I have begun to consciously develop a better understanding of the communication I pick up during these experiences, and especially when I am sketching. I say begun to understand, because this is an ongoing process of learning to interpret the language of the right-brain intuition, which appears to interface with a stream of collective knowledge. And, through teaching and sharing intuitive and shamanic art, I learn more about this amazing creative stream every day!

Archaeologists tell us that art in the form of cave paintings and carvings began at least 40,000 years ago, and recent findings suggest it may be even further back than this. As a child, these ancient works of art seemed very mysterious to me, and I wondered what kind of magic they contained that caused me to get goose-bumps just by looking at pictures of them. It struck me as significant that mankind was the only species on Earth with the ability to create art – and I mean create, and not just copy. What was early man doing, I wondered? Was he simply drawing what he could see? Was he creating decoration because it made him feel good to live with it? Did he just enjoy making art for its own sake, or could there be other deeper reasons?

I think it may have been my grandfather that first gave me the idea that cave paintings were perhaps done to represent what these ancient cave-dwellers needed; that they drew a bison on the cave wall to physically bring the bison to the tribe, so they could eat it. That this practice was in fact a ritual intended to conjure up the bison by using the painting as an artistic prayer, or magical spell. It was an idea I never questioned; it just seemed right.

In the same way, I have heard it suggested that the stone carvings of the pregnant Goddess found in the caves, were perhaps carved when they wanted to increase tribal numbers and used to 'wish' pregnancies onto the tribal woman. Also cave paintings have been found recently of animals, thought not thought to be useful for food, but rather to manifest the qualities and strength of the animals displayed. Once again this was the art of manifestation, creating what was wanted, using the power of artistic representation.

So it seems on a deep and even subconscious level, we always knew that by visualising our goal we could achieve it physically. By actually creating the image, mankind believed he would achieve it. And we still know today that the best way of achieving something is to believe that we can.

This idea sat well with me on a deep level, something I had always known, and took it for granted in my every day life. But the more I considered it, the more it came to the surface, and within the context of the work I now do, it becomes more and more obvious to me that cave paintings were actually our first Mandalas. Then in the last few years, as if more evidence were needed, I heard a lecture given by the late Ian Xen Lungold talking about the importance of art in his presentation of the Mayan Tun Calendar – see Chapter 6 – I am now convinced that the true nature of cave paintings was Mandalic – containers for intention energy.

This idea also follows the premise of 'like attracts like', perhaps an old wives' tale, as my grandmother used to say; yet one that has survived the test of time, and certainly one that is very popular today under the label, The Law of Attraction.

Understanding how this 'magic' works, as well as what prevents it, is the key to using it consistently and successfully. As you will see throughout this book, art is a magical ingredient here, but is it the finished artwork that holds the magical connection, the process of its creation, the person creating it, the person interacting with it, or all these factors put together? These are the questions we will explore further, and we will reach our conclusions not only by looking back at history and tradition, but by exploring the workings of Mandalas through the personal experiences and connections shared in this book, as well as the opportunity to create your own new experiences.

So let's look back at Eastern traditions, particularly in Tibet. The intent and the ritual of Mandala making is often more important than the finished Mandala itself. Tibetan coloured sand Mandalas are created meticulously grain-by-grain. In training the mind to focus purely on a single intention, Mandala-making is in this instance used as a powerful aid to attaining a focused mind, and thereby inner peace.

In Tibetan tradition it is considered a blessing to even see a completed Mandala, as it conveys a deep activation of wholeness, promoting healing and peace. The destruction of these sand Mandalas also has a powerful purpose, a reminder of the impermanence of life and the practice of non-attachment. The coloured sands that have made up the Mandala are swept up into an urn and then scattered into the river –a way of spreading its healing powers to the whole world through the connectedness of water. This ritual is offered as a sacrificial or transformational rite to Mother Earth to re-energise the environment and universe.

The Taoist 'yin-yang' symbol is a Mandala that represents opposition as well as cooperation, male and female, intellect and intuition equally; therefore symbolising a balanced and peaceful way of being. The Mandala I recently created to evoke PEACE resembles this symbol, yet surprisingly not through any conscious plan on my part. You'll begin to understand what I really mean by that, only when you experience making your own Mandalas using the guidance in Chapter 4.

You will also see in the feedback given in Appendix 2, there have been mixed reactions to this PEACE Mandala; some people finding it calming, while others finding it extremely challenging! Accepting peace can be challenging to the ego, especially when we realise that to achieve peace outside in the world, we must first develop it inside our own head. And to do that, we must take personal responsibility for turning down the loud voice of the ego and embracing the change that is created within.

In Indian Tantra, the Mandala is a tool for alchemy as well as meditation. It helps to bring feelings and visions forward from the space within, to the world outside. The Bindu is said to be the centre point within, the focal point of the universe – the ultimate point from which everything emerges, and to which everything is directed back. The Bindu is without beginning or end, and is neither positive nor negative. It is also said to radiate waves of vibration or sound from itself. Therefore, as a singularity, the Bindu Mandala represents potential – simultaneous evolution and termination, intention and response, as well as activity and stillness. The Bindu is the first dot before duality was born, and a return pathway to enlightenment and oneness.

Some Tantric Mandalas are created for the embodiment of deities, making a portal, or bridge for energy to pass through from one dimension to another; alchemically realising the energy of deity through the Bindu into this physical realm.

This concept applies to drawing images of deities, saints, angels and spirit guides; I had used it intuitively for years before I even knew what I was doing. I have now learned to draw with conscious intent, utilising this Tantric idea of a conscious energy flow from active to receptive energy points, and it has stimulated some very interesting feedback on the after-effects of these connections. The Mandalic intent of these drawing has been so 'alive' that clients continue to receive energy through these drawings, well after the reading is finished, offering both a physical and mental reminder of the connection that was established and evoking the energy of that guiding energy again and again when requested in the future.

The concept of the Mandala has been expanded to cover a wide range of different ideas over the years. The tradition of Mandala-making can be found in ancient cultures, the methodology handed down over thousands of years and remaining consistent over millennia through their shape and form, often circular or geometric.

Here, however, we will be open to explore Mandalas from a new and freer perspective, which allows for individual expression and without fear of a 'wrong way'. This freedom of thought allows us to flow and create our intention in a way that feels right, intuitively using either free form or following the tradition of geometry, dependent on our purpose. It becomes a way of embracing change with the new energy available to us now, still using the stability of tried and tested foundations as a guide.

So how does it work? As human beings, when we focus on something, we connect and co-create with a flow of conscious energy; we feel it on different levels of awareness. This flow of energy is what sets things into motion, and when it is sustained or repeated it causes things to manifest. Although believing this fully may require a major shift in understanding for us, it is this shift we need to make in order to make a huge difference to our lives. We need to come to know how we collectively create our lives, our world, and the very nature of our reality.

Mandalas are a physical tool that will help us to make this shift, allowing us to experience how we can actually affect our reality by adding the dots and joining them up. In very practical ways that we can monitor and validate on an ongoing basis ... and when we acknowledge that we can connect, we truly will!

In my experience, the secret to manifesting is to invest an

optimum amount of energy so that it can flow effortlessly from source. Investing too little energy will not fuel the intention; this occurs when we lose focus. Investing too much causes a back-surge. This back-surge occurs when we are too attached to the outcome. It causes fear, and fear of failure prevents energy from flowing towards the original goal; reversing it back to create the opposite of was intended. The energy flows back towards failure simply because our attention is unwittingly placed on failure in our fear of its consequences.

We've all heard the saying 'Where intention goes, energy flows' and this is true, however it isn't the complete picture. If I were going to make an addition it would be, 'Where intention goes energy flows, but fear creates lack, as it turns the flow back!'

I was very privileged to have my understanding of this processed heightened through a real-life experience, when I did a parachute jump many years ago. My squash club decided to do a parachute jump to raise money for charity. We were given our sponsorship forms and people pledged money for our cause. Finally the big day arrived, and we set off for Headcorn in Kent, where our adventure was to take place.

After the required two days of training – and many bruises later – we were prepared… at least we thought we were. Finally, sitting on the floor of the small aircraft 1,200 ft high in the air, it was too late to back out now. The instructor called for our attention and pointed out a tiny white cross, marked in the centre of a field that seemed to me way, way down below the plane in another reality! Shouting to be heard over the thunderous engine noise and wind crashing in through the open door, he explained, 'I need you to land as close to that white cross as you possibly can, okay? Keep your eyes on the cross… remember you will always travel in the direction you're facing and faster with the wind behind you. Pulling the right toggle turns you right, left toggle to turn left… got it? We'll be there in two minutes. Good luck!'

Eyebrows were raised and we were all deathly silent, faces drained of blood as we realised that we were about to jump out of that doorway and into thin air.

'Okay we're here. If you're drifting away from the field, turn until you can see the cross again, remember to smile at the camera on the way out...okay, one at a time, come here.... Ready in 5... 4...'

Jill nudged me and pointed at a small copse of trees at the top of the field as she moved to take her position in the doorway. 'I hope I don't land in there!' she laughed nervously.

'....3....2....1 GO, GO, GO!' A firm hand on the back and next thing plummeting towards Earth! So we all left the aircraft in one way or another; some jumped and others were pushed out before they changed their mind. The five seconds of free fall before the canopy opening was the biggest rush, every muscle in my body clenched...

"One thousand, two thousand, three thou-ooooooh shhhh-hhhit!"

Canopy opened, relief ensued.

'Thank You!'

... Time to unclench, relax, and enjoy the rest of the ride down, with one eye on that white cross. Jill, however, was so keen to avoid landing in the trees, that she kept looking to make sure she was far enough away from them. Not a good idea to focus on where you don't want to go! As she got closer and closer to the ground, she became so transfixed on the trees, she lost sight of her target ... she landed in a tree, hung up on one of the branches!

We've all experienced something like this at some stage, albeit not as dramatic and obvious as Jill's hang-up, but the metaphor applies to many situations. Sometimes things just don't seem to go well no matter how much we try. Often the more effort we put in, the more difficult it becomes. So, what can we do? How can we discern how much effort is too much? And how can we overcome the fear of failure that causes a reverse flow? Well, the answer is within our control because there is a reason why energy flows one way or another, and the good news is, we are the reason!

This book will help you to understand your flow and help you take control of your thoughts so that you can connect and allow energy to free flow from divinity, rather than become stuck by trying to make energy flow from your ego-self, which is too far away from its source. It will guide you to create powerful Mandalas, even if you can't draw. You will learn to discern the active from the inactive, the energetic from the flat, the powerful from the weak, and what you'll need to do inside your head in order to make them work!

Chapter 2

Right-Brain Divinity

"The meaning of prayer is that I want to evoke that Divinity within me."
~ Gandhi

Is it possible to evoke divinity by simply praying? Certainly there have been people who could make us feel we are in the presence of divinity, just by being in their company. Their peace and calmness able to radiate all around them, even changing the feeling of the atmosphere... but even if we do believe it is possible for someone with a 'spiritual' lifestyle such as Gandhi, Mother Theresa or the Dalai Lama to evoke this feeling of divinity, we mostly don't believe 'normal' people can evoke it. Well at least not in a sustainable way, because the second we may think we are connected to something that feels divine, either through prayer or meditation, an unhelpful thought gatecrashes our mind, and blows the whole divinity thing clean out of the water. So what causes this? For your information, that will be our logical thinking left-brain! Hence the saying EGO = 'Easing God Out'!

However, times do change, and science can sometimes come up with proof that our human brain is capable of incredible things. When this happens, it is very exciting and is a signal that we may well be on a schedule of changing consciousness. From what I have gathered through my study of the way our brain and mind works, our right-brain hemisphere can commune with wisdom beyond mere left-brain logic, and is also aware of the bigger picture. This consciousness comes forward when we enter an altered state of awareness, which means when the left-brained judgmental ego is 'turned down' or even when, at times, it goes 'off line'. Only then is the right-brain able to provide insights that can be remembered and interpreted when we return to our normal state of awareness.

Neurologists may well say it's not as simple as that, because various areas of the brain are multi-functional. In fact, the whole brain has plasticity, meaning it can change and rewire itself depending on circumstances. Whilst of course the brain is very complicated and we don't understand exactly how all our thinking cells work – including the many thinking cells that have been discovered in our heart – I use this concept of left-brain (LB) and right-brain (RB) to highlight the fact that we have two distinctive styles of thought that are in conflict with each other, intuitive thought v logical thought; wherever they are located, and even if they can move around in the whole body! The location is secondary to the process of interaction.

Dr Jill Bolte-Taylor, a Harvard-trained and published neuro-anatomist recently added credence to this idea, when her own left-brain chatter was abruptly silenced. In her case it was when she was unfortunate enough to witness herself having a stroke. It turned out that Dr Jill had a golf-ball sized blood clot pressing on the left hemisphere of her brain, which gradually closed down her ability to function logically.

The right-brain was then free to function single-handedly with surprising results. Dr Jill talks about witnessing a connection to oneness that sounds like divinity itself, and she has remained a changed woman some eight years after this experience. You can watch the 18-minute video [5] of her detailing how she felt as her consciousness moved from one side of her brain to the other as she struggled to function logically on the left-side, and found herself unconcerned and experiencing divinity on the right-side.

She sums up at the end of her talk, 'So who are we? We are the life force power of the universe, with manual dexterity and two cognitive minds. And we have the power to choose, moment by moment, who and how we want to be in the world. Right here right now, I can step into the consciousness of my right hemisphere where we are the – I am – the life force power of the universe, and the life force power of the 50 trillion beautiful molecular geniuses that make up my form; at one with all that is. Or I can choose to step into the consciousness of my left hemisphere, where I become a single individual; a solid, separate from the flow, separate from you. I am Dr Jill Bolte- Taylor, intellectual, neuro-anatomist. These are the "we" inside of me. Which would you choose? Which do you choose? And when? I believe that the more time we spend choosing to run the deep inner peace circuitry of our right hemispheres, the more peace we will project into the world and the more peaceful our planet will be. And I thought that was an idea worth spreading!'

Accounts such as this validate that we really have inside connection to the wisdom contained in the stream of consciousness that I refer to as the Omniversal Mind (OM) and that Science refers to as the quantum energy field. I can, and do, experience switching out of my left-brain consciousness, fortunately not because of a stroke, but through using sketching and automatic writing when I switch into the right-side; so I can personally relate to what Dr Jill describes in this video, when I too am in this very different awareness of reality. I have come to realise that when the partnership of our own brain hemispheres can cooperate, rather than compete, we can achieve much more than with logic alone. And we can with practice make it happen.

I firstly began to realise the significance of this idea when I discovered the work of Nobel Prize winner Dr Roger Woolcote Sperry [6], who states 'both the left and the right hemisphere may be conscious simultaneously in different, even in mutually conflicting, mental experiences that run along in parallel.'

Since then it has been reinforced many times in my own work, and now again through Dr Jill Bolte-Taylor's first-hand experience. When her left-brain tried to take over every time it came back online, it fearfully told her she had a problem and must get help. Yet the right-brain was mindful of the connectivity and oneness of us all, and she could not see where her body ended and where the space around her began. She was calm and had no fear of death, knowing that death was not the end.

Since this inner experience, Dr Jill has concluded that the majority of people operate on what she says is an 85%-15% left-brain dominated way during normal waking consciousness, rather than balance of rational logic and intuition.

I have experienced this conflict in myself, and in others many times and can again relate to what she says. I notice this left-brain dominance when I teach people to make their own Mandalas. Their left-brain disbelief kicks in to sabotage what's happening, mostly through fear of losing control. This makes logical sense, because from the left-brain's point of view, why would you be happy with only 50% control or less if you already have 85%?

Although recently I have realised that the balance is slowly shifting toward the right-brain, certainly in the groups I am privileged to teach, and I believe this will continue the more aware we become. When we realise that 50% of creativity and infinite wisdom is more valuable than 85% of knowledge, however clever we think we are!

As technology speeds up, there is a sense that time is going faster, causing us to experience more stress, anxiety, fears and phobias. These are all symptoms of left-brain dominance, which triggers our normal fight-or-flight response, but making war or running away into alcohol, drugs or apathy just isn't working. And the quicker technology and creativity evolve, the more we won't cope in the old way of being. There's only one place left to go if we want to survive, and that is into using our right-brain intuition more; to literally step out of our current mindset and enter the magic.

That's why it's important when we make Mandalas that we

call upon the 'magic' mix of right-brain feelings and left-brain words in order to create a balanced Mandala and stop the internal sabotage. My most successful Mandalas have been a combination of both sides, the verbal and non-verbal expression. The dynamic of the energy of 'two or more' plays its part in expanding the flow.

When we can learn to use the right-brain side of ourselves to lead, we naturally increase our ability to focus our attention. Once we can use focused attention, even for short bursts, we can connect and create powerful Mandalas. Even during the process of deciding on and contemplating a purpose for our Mandala, our ability to manifest grows naturally too, as the clarity of what we need to achieve dawns on us.

The easiest way to notice when we are using our right-brain to lead, is that we can focus our attention easily. Time flies and one aspect of our activity melds seamlessly into the next without effort, without thought, without ego. And here's the bonus – it's actually fun and we enjoy ourselves. The right side can have fun and laugh as it experiences, whilst the left can only talk about how funny it is!

It's one of the most illuminating and rewarding parts of the workshops and retreats I lead. I am regularly delighted by participants who at first say they have no idea what they wish to create, and then go on to produce powerful pieces of artwork that help them to activate their goals. I also see participants, who previously think they can't draw, putting intense thoughts and feelings into their Mandalas as they draw, and then are delighted when they learn that other people can connect to this energy in their artwork. So I always say that the more we acknowledge what is happening in this process, the stronger our connection and the better intenders we become. We literally journey into the dimension of art.

Dr Sperry's work showed that activities such as creating, dancing, music, sports, colour awareness, are generally a right-brain activity. It was my own sketching experiences that first led me to recognise that right-brain art was a key for me to commune with this amazing energy. Right-brain art is very different from left-brain art, in that there is no plan, no control, no trying; simply intent. Using this awareness helps me to quieten down the left-brain so that I can bring forward accurate information that I wouldn't logically know, even about people who are deceased, which suggests the far-reaching potential of working with our right-brain. I am now, more than ever, coming to terms with the fact that our right-brain feminine aspect can evoke a stream of conscious divinity, which 'knows' everything, or at least accesses this knowledge, and can offer us extraordinary experiences within that connection.

Using this connection, I was inspired to produced a range of six Mandalas embedded with helpful, if not essential qualities of Love, Light, Peace, Joy, Healing and my tongue-in-cheek favourite Enlighten or light-heartedness. This range was inspired by the need to bring these qualities into my own life as well as the desire to share them with others. I put as much focused attention into them as I could, and allowed the energy to connect and flow between the poles – and it did flow in a big way! It was a wonderful experience and I took great satisfaction from the whole process; from the preparation to finally interacting with them.

Once these Mandalas were complete, I decided to conduct some experiments with them to see if and how they could affect other people as well as myself. My experiments were done over a period of several months where I asked volunteers to interact with the Mandalas that I gave them. The experimenters were asked to display the Mandala as screen-savers on their computer and on their mobile phone. This turned out to be a very powerful way to view them, as not only was the experimenter exposed to them repeatedly, even when away from home, but the light behind the image also projects the energy into the eyes and into the space around the Mandala. So not only do we send out our consciousness to look at them, they send their energy out to enter inside of us.

Experimenters were also asked to print the Mandala to hang as artwork on auspicious walls according to [7]Vaastu or Feng Shui placement areas in the home. I display my images on a digital photo-frame in my lounge, where they project their connection outwards from the backlight. We can aim to take full advantage of the energy of placement and position according to ancient tradition.

I also printed them onto coasters and place mats, again making use of another very powerful way to interact with a Mandala; imbibing the water and food so the energy moves inside your whole system. Looking back, tradition tells us about the value of Holy water, and teaches us to bless our food. Further to this the Japanese scientist Dr Masuro Emoto is doing experiments on water[8] that show visually, by monitoring the designs of ice crystals formed, what changes may be possible simply through the way we behave and speak around water – as well as how we treat water.

So remember this when you create your Mandala: it's your feelings rather than your thoughts that matter as you focus. We can all feel the energy of focused attention on various levels, and some people are naturally more sensitive to it than others. When we watch a Mandala and feel it reflecting back at us we make a connection. I believe, as the saying goes, that the eyes are the windows to the soul, and if we explore the idea of a window, it offers a view from inside out as well as from the outside in!

Exploring this focus, experiments done on the sense of being stared at, show that energy somehow radiates from the person staring to the subject being stared at, indicating further that we can and do affect reality by simply observing it. Rupert Sheldrake reports on this work in his book *The Sense of Being Stared At* [9] which includes reports from zoom lens cameramen and surveillance experts, who say that it is important not to focus too much on the people they are watching, as they tend to look round, exactly the basis of this research.

So we now have some proof that we send out 'something' when we focus upon it. Currently science cannot measure whatever this connection is with instruments, but they can definitely see the affect it has on the experimenters.

I have also added some feedback at the end of this chapter, which shares experiences from my volunteers as they interacted with the Mandala I imbibed with JOY. Agreement between them shows evidence that some kind of change occurs in how they feel. Of course we cannot assume this will be the case for everyone, but I have included a coloured image of the 'Joy' Mandala in on my website at www.psychicartworks.com/joy.html so that you can do your own experiments too[10]. It doesn't matter how many people tell you about their experience, until you experience the mystery for yourself, you cannot really know. A deeper understanding is always possible through direct experience. So as you first look at this Mandala, witness how you feel, and note any response you may or may not have, simply for your own exploration. Feel how it would be to send out your awareness, to explore the image, and then allow the image to enter within you. Left-brain exploring outwards – what's there? Right-brain exploring inwards – how does it affect you?

Feedback From The JOY Mandala Experimenters

I just finished my first day of the Mandala experiment. I can't believe how great I feel! Even though I've been having a disagreement with my boyfriend (which is disturbing my JOY) I still feel wonderful. My water that I placed on the coaster is delicious too!

*   *   *

I would say that it took between 4-5 days before there was any discernible effects or benefits. The first notable effect was of a cognitive nature – I had the feeling that I was retaining information more easily, and being more articulate and confident in public speaking, enhancing knowledge transfer...

* * *

As I looked at the image I couldn't believe it, it was exactly what I needed! I have been feeling down for ages. Unhappy with work, unfulfilled in my relationships and also with life in general – not to mention being ill constantly and having no energy. When I first saw it I instantly had a sense of feeling joyful as I looked into it, but I soon dipped back down again as I realised that an image couldn't really help me. Yet over the next few days I actually did feel better, and although I don't understand how I continue to feel better now – how weird is that?

* * *

There are recurring periods where there is a feeling of energized physicality. I catch myself needlessly running up stairs, and not really being in a hurry, have to consciously turn it down a bit. This is sporadic, but discernible and unusual.

* * *

There has been a more positive blanket effect of calming. If I let myself go, I seem to naturally gravitate towards the pessimistic. I would say that the only other personal practice that has generated a similar sense of focus and well-being has been meditation, but with the perceived 'lift' from a good meditation being instantaneous, the benefits from this experiment seem to have been ongoing, more of a slow burner!

* * *

My initial reaction was, wow, how beautiful! I immediately felt uplifted and joyful.
I believe the JOY Mandala is really helping me! I feel much more upbeat lately. I definitely notice a change in my attitude since I begun using it!

* * *

I feel I have this inner sense of joy and calm and that something truly wonderful is about to happen any day! I am also a hypnotherapist so I definitely notice many subtle changes in a subconscious level.

* * *

My sense was of being even more optimistic than normal; the image made me smile whenever I caught sight of it – the colors are certainly cheerful, happy and joyous. What a difference to be reminded of positive things in life so refreshing, The cup is definitely half full, how I could ever doubt it, and if I do in moments of madness I will just look at JOY!

Chapter 3

Experience The Mystery

The most beautiful thing we can experience is the mysterious.
It is the source of all true art and science.
~ Albert Einstein

I believe the Mandala's true purpose through history has been mystified by 'the chosen few' who have used them efficiently but often in secret, passed down from guru to student, shaman to initiate, behind closed doors. I believe this 'know how' can be brought to light now by tapping into the stream of consciousness available through the quantum energy field; by using the right-brain hemisphere as explained earlier.

Mandalas are gateways to commune with a powerful force that we all can learn to connect with directly now. They are part of our heritage, something for us all to understand and enjoy, the ultimate embodiment of essence, a magnification of our energy and connection to our source. My intention is therefore to reestablish the Mandala as a vehicle to connect to source, to carry and also radiate our intentions for as long as it takes them to manifest and also to help us train our minds by showing us the rewards that the mind can achieve.

Using the Mandala in this way allows us to focus for short periods of time just while we are making the Mandala, rather than have to develop the ability to focus every day for hours and hours at a time, before we see any results. I've used my own practice, as well as my experience in helping others, to formulate the best ways to create Mandalas that work. This chapter and the next will therefore offer you the means to directly experience this mystery for yourself.

There are four phases to a Mandala:
1. The Intentional phase
2. The Creation phase
3. The Completed Mandala
4. The Interactive phase

There are five qualities involved in a Mandala, and each one adds its energy to the whole, making a powerful marriage using the 'Law of Two or More'[11]

– when two or more come together with like minds, divinity is evoked.
1. The giver or teacher
2. The intention
3. The location
4. The timing
5. The receiver or student

There are six forms of Mandala
Our senses direct messages between the outer world of the physical and the inner world of the mind; all of the senses receive and deliver messages to consciousness through these various forms.

1. Visual Mandala: seeing 2-dimensional, 3-dimensional and 4-dimensional art
2. Audible Mandala: hearing sound sculpture, chanting, music and mantra
3. Consumable Mandala: tasting food and / or drink, medicine and remedies
4. Aromatic Mandala: smelling pheromones, incense, perfume and fragrance
5. Tactile Mandala: touching texture, objects, toys, massage and

contact

6. Multi-Sensory Mandala: multi-dimensional

The Four Phases

1. **The intention** is the first phase, and it is the most important. It often takes the longest period of time to formulate and contemplate, as this foundation is key to knowing what we really need – in line with the bigger picture or divine plan. It helps us to focus our thoughts on what we want to achieve, and often helps us to see how much energy we have been giving away to the things we don't want. Clarity at last!

2. **Creation** is the second phase and can take five minutes, five days, five years or even more. It is often the most pleasing phase as it takes us into our creative right-brain hemisphere where things are light hearted, enjoyable and where we can connect within a stream of knowing. However, there are times when the creative process of the Mandala is done simply for student practise, as a form of meditation to achieve peace, calm and discipline within the mind; to help us relax into the flow.

3. **Completion** is the third phase, and an important part of the process. The Mandala must 'feel' right. If the Mandala doesn't feel alive when it is complete it probably isn't potent enough to manifest its intent. We know on a deep level when this is the case, and if it's not right we can always create another until it does feel right. You will feel as if the energy is 'alive' and connected because it will communicate to you, and in this awareness, practice makes perfect!

4. **The interaction** phase is dependant on the intention of the Mandala. For example, ongoing interaction is key for a manifestation, but undesirable for a clearing Mandala, which should be burned or transformed in some other way. This can

be anything from having it somewhere you can see it, to actually taking your consciousness into it through staring at it.

The Five Qualities
1. The Giver or Teacher
The qualities apparent in the creator will affect the Mandala. Self-made Mandalas are self-empowering and ultimately best, and you know what you intended to put into them! However, a good level of focused attention is required to make a potent Mandala. So to begin with you may wish to use a Mandala that has been made for a specific purpose for you, and that feels 'right' to you. You can also choose one that you participate in making along with an experienced Mandala-maker or teacher who will help you to enter the flow; or else choose one that draws you to it – one that chooses you!

2. The Intention itself
The quality of our intention depends on clarity and focus – preparation is key here. Spending time contemplating the intention we wish to hold in our Mandala is beneficial. The way we think and what we say doesn't always portray what we really mean! Many of my sessions consist of spending much of the time setting the most helpful intention, and deciding on which type of Mandala people require – before we even begin the creation process. If the way we think about and talk about our intentions is unclear, we would be well advised to remember that unclear intentions do not make potent Mandalas. In fact they can create unintentional Mandalas, which can manifest what we don't really want! Precise, simple and clear intentions work best. Always mention words that describe what you want, and not words that describe what you don't want! In other words, no, to losing weight; Yes, to being lighter.

3. **Location**

Where the Mandala is made and where is it placed affect its qualities; the power of place, obviously the energy in central London is very different to the energy in the depths of a forest. So where you create the Mandala will have an affect on it. It is best to create the Mandala in a place where you feel comfortable. Add to the good vibration of a room by burning incense and / or playing relaxing music, or choose a power place outside; follow your intuition for this. When you decide on what you want to achieve with your Mandala, you will naturally be drawn to the ideal place to create it.

The placement of the finished Mandala also affects it qualities. I suggest you position your Mandala where your intuition guides you, somewhere you can see it; you will know where to place it by the way it makes you feel. Once positioned, you can still move it if you feel strongly that you should, even if you don't know why. Also you should re-evaluate a Mandala if three months has elapsed without significant results manifesting. In this case, you can change position – or you may even want to make a new Mandala.

If you really cannot decide where to place the Mandala, you can use the Guidance Notes at the end of chapter 4, which are based on Feng Shui to check the most auspicious position in line with the intention. As you look at the room-plan in fig 2 the main entrance to the room would be anywhere along the bottom line so that the Wealth corner is at the far left side.

4. **Timing**

Mandalas can be made that can change our view of the past and thereby change how we feel in the present, helping us to be more powerful in the future. This can be tricky to understand, simply because time itself is not easy to understand. In the left-brain world we understand a sequential time-line, but in the right-brain world there is a much bigger picture – even beyond a sequential

Fig 2

Abundance	Admiration	Relationship
Wealth	Reputation	Love
Family	Health	Creativity
Stability	Well Being	Children
Skill	Career	Travel
Wisdom	Life Path	Helpful People

time-line – that we don't yet understand!

Even so, we do know that different periods of time have different energy; just think about the world five years ago compared with how it is now. Also think of the difference between spring and autumn. But when it comes to the calendar and clock, if you really think about it, which Cosmic Law states a minute is a minute, or a year is a year? Well, it's logic we are working with – for now – so I use the ancient art of Ayurveda[12] for my guidance in this. I was taught if you do something every day for a month, it becomes a habit. If that's the conclusion of human behaviour for over 3,000 years plus, who am I to argue? So I apply this to Manifestation Mandalas. If I look at a Mandala every day for a month, I know it's had an effect and I am ready for my tangible result any day!

The time when we actually make the Mandala also has an

influence on its quality. Astrology can guide us here in terms of auspicious dates, although personally I prefer to pay attention to how I feel at different times of the day or year, and trust my inner guidance. Timing is a huge subject, but I'll briefly offer a couple of concepts I sometimes use. However, do remember that a Mandala done at any time is better than one not done at all!

At times I pay attention to the phases of the moon. As it waxes – the two weeks from the new moon growing towards fullness – I use this time to create Mandalas for new beginnings and to promote growth. As it wanes, I use this time to create Mandalas for clearing, also for reducing unwanted thoughts or habits, for learning to focus and for disciplining the mind.

I also follow the principles of Ayurveda for timing [13]. There are three energies described in Ayurveda that affect everything in the world. They cannot be seen, because they are not physical, but they can be observed. Much like the wind, only their effects can be witnessed. The three energies or *doshas* (Sanskrit) are *Kapha, Pitta* and *Vata*.

Each have different qualities, and at certain times those qualities have more influence than others. The trick is to pick a time when the dosha that best helps your intention is most influential.

The three qualities are related to the elements:

Vata is like air and space, the dosha for movement, transition or change, fast speed, often fleeting, therefore good for a drastic change with a fast result, but not long lasting.
Pitta is like fire and water, the dosha for transformation, balance or passion. Energetic and fairly stable, it is good for transformation of anything you wish to build on.
Kapha is like water and earth, the dosha for stability, grounding or connection. Moving at slow speed with the ability to sustain, it is ideal for security or stability although results may take a longer time to manifest. Slow, steady but sure is the key quality here.

The dominant periods occur for approximately four-hour periods in rotation at different times of day, note slightly different times in winter than summer.

Vata around sunrise and sunset – 4am to 8am and 4pm to 8pm

Pitta around midday – 12 noon to 4pm and midnight to 4am

Kapha mid-morning and later evening – 8am to 12 noon and 8pm to midnight

The doshas are also are predominant during different seasons, dependant on the climate.

Pitta – hottest (and wet)

Vata – dry, windy, changeover between hot and cold

Kapha – cold and damp (or snow)

5. The Receiver or Student

It is helpful if the recipient or student of the Mandala is open to receiving the affect, although this quality of openness is not essential. Mandalas affect all without prejudice on the level of subconscious. In other words, if the quality of the intent, energy and belief of the creator is well focused, and the Mandala is 'alive', what will manifest does not require the observer to believe, simply just to see the Mandala regularly. This is an important point to note, and is connected to the Law of Mass Consciousness.

The Six Physical Forms Of Mandala are

1. **Visual Mandalas** come in several forms both as 2-dimensional and 3-dimensional art. They are sometimes circular or geometrical.

The yellow smiley face icon is probably the most well known visual Mandala in the western world, designed to reproduce the energy of a smile, which it does perfectly and as you can see it often generates a smile in the observer.

See Fig 3

Fig 3

And talking of three dimensions, did you ever wonder what was on the back of a smiley icon... a plain yellow circle? Apparently not, I'll leave it to your imagination to picture a smiley moon and create an even broader smile! ☺

Photographs and paintings are good ways to display Mandalas. They bring energy to a room, as interior designers know very well – so be aware of these types of Mandala you display in your home. Desolate landscapes, images of loneliness or disturbing images can imprint your space.

If you are not feeling relaxed at home, take a look around and feel what is going on. Your home is also a container of energy. Creating visual Mandalas to hang in certain areas of the home help increase their manifestation affect. If you are not clear where in your room is the best place to hang your Mandala, you can be guided by the Feng Shui system for placement.

Greetings cards are thoughtful ways to send visual Mandalas to people you care for. A healing Mandala sent to someone who is unwell is very beneficial on different levels of awareness. Cards can often catch our eye, but do we stop to think about why that is, or do we simply choose them on a subconscious level without thinking why? Greeting cards work in the 4th dimension of time as well. The timing just as important as the message of the card, we would all appreciate the right card at the right time.

Clothing, as my fashion background has taught me, has a huge visual impact on the observer. Colour, design and logo all contain a specific energy that you actually walk around inside. We all know that some favourite clothes make us feel really good, but do we know how and why? Our clothing is part of our personal Mandala – more in Chapter 8.

Printed sticky label Mandalas are great to have around the home and workplace. I stick them on products I buy that seem to have fallen through my awareness net! In other words, don't focus on 'anti wrinkle' face cream, which instils the idea of wrinkles into your subconscious. Instead choose to add a label of love or joy onto the face cream. It definitely works, as everyone says I look great for 142! Hmmm. Many common labels have negative messages and are in direct opposition to what is wanted, without us even realising. Although I must say lately I have been noticing some very interesting adverts that seem to be sending out positive messages to the subconscious. Perhaps the brand designers are becoming more aware, or maybe it's that our mass consciousness is now shifting.

Clocks and watches are useful ways to display Mandalas because we check the time so often. With a little effort you can create your own or adapt the ones you have.

Mirrors, too, make great bases for Mandalas, doubling the power through reflection.

Finally, screen savers for computers, digital photo frames and mobile phones can make full use of the latest technology of vision and sound in a very positive way.

2. Sound Mandalas

These often take the form of chants, mantras, resolutions, tones or pieces of music, written to evoke the feeling and emotions of the theme; often achieved in film music, by talented composers.

These musical messages can accompany slogans in advertising as a memorable 'sting' – a short catchy tune – or can be used as attention-grabbing frequencies and tones to tell us to get out of the way of the emergency services.

Sound Mandalas created on Tibetan singing bowls, gongs and voice by sound healers, achieve beneficial results, bringing both emotional and physical healing to individuals. During sound ceremonies in workshops[14] that I offer when working with sound healer Ian Dale, the participants can also create a visual Mandala while bathing in these healing sounds; this adds another dimension to the energy, and acts as a container of the energy that people take home for use afterwards.

You can experience this for yourself by attending a Mandala-making workshop, but you could also get an idea of it by listening to Tracks 6 and 7 on the companion CD to *The Art Of Being ... Psychic*. This CD contains powerful sound Mandalas specifically to trigger the intuitive right-side of the brain. Often people's reaction, especially to using track 7 is 'I can't think straight when it's on!'

Of course, that is the point; it switches you into right-brain non-thinking mode! Listen, and do nothing as you listen; just feel what's happening. This is very beneficial to listen to when Mandala-making. There is also a short sample available on my website. Finally, our own voice, the sound of our breathing, and even our heart beating is part of our personal Mandala.

3. **Consumable Mandalas**

Food, glorious food; there's nothing quite like it! Mandalas in the form of food or drink are taken in and digested inside the body, and so the effect is more physically obvious. The saying "we are what we eat," holds some truth. The work of researcher and peace activist Dr Masaru Emoto has brought to light the idea that we can actually affect water with words. And as approximately 75% of the physical matter in our body is water, a healing Mandala used to affect water is very beneficial. The Mandala of 'Love' on my website can be used freely as a coaster, to add love to your drinking water. Taste the difference!

Food cooked while thinking loving thoughts carries the energy of those loving thoughts into it. Again you can taste the difference. A meal prepared and cooked with love and arranged on a plate in an attractive way, with balanced colours and textures and then finally blessed, is a powerful Mandala indeed. No wonder home-cooked food, made by a loving mother, is by far the most enjoyable.

So a carefully prepared meal is a Mandala. It generates the energy of the food and also the intention of the cook; be aware of what you eat, who cooks for you, and what you are thinking about when you cook. If you cook with love, it can be tasted... delicious![15] And remember, sending your blessing and thanks to food before you eat it, no matter who cooked it, adds positive energy.

4. Aromatic Mandalas

Aromas carry a powerful energy and messages through 'thin air'. Just think of pheromones – nature's subconscious messengers. If you thought water and food were good carriers of energy, let's consider air and space... it gets everywhere. Science tells us that approximately 80% of our physical body is simply space and air. This being so, imagine how powerful fragrance is as a healing and balancing aid. No wonder religions have used incense in their buildings for centuries. Scented candles have also become popular as a way of creating a relaxing, meditative atmosphere.

Just remember how you feel when you smell your favourite smell; be it food, like homemade fresh bread, or a favourite perfume; and even how much more pleasing it is when the container or meal is pleasing to look at as well. A Mandala in a bottle or on a plate!

The power of smell is more widely used today than ever

before. Oil containing carefully chosen essential oils mixed while thinking of positive intentions of love and healing makes the oil perfect for a fantastic healing bath or a massage – this is aromatherapy.

Lastly, in terms of aromas I want to mention flowers. Women in particular love to receive flowers as a token of love. I know a wonderful florist who loves arranging flowers, and any that she creates for me seem to last longer; they also attract lots of compliments from my visitors. A floral Mandala made with 'Love' is a combination of visual shape, colour and aroma. Just perfect!

5. A Tactile Mandala

I would say the teddy bear is probably the most popular cuddly Mandala. The soft furry touch that carries a message for cuddling and brings comfort and healing to many children. One could understand how a handmade teddy, if created while thinking loving thoughts, would be an even greater comfort for a restless child. Even an old blanket will often bring the same comfort, and is carried around endlessly by some young ones; only surrendered unwillinglly when mother finally manages to kidnap and wash it. The energy and comforting message is perhaps washed away.

The Mandala of touch is an interesting one. The quality of touch varies enormously. Often touch is thought of as sensing what's outside in an effort to explore the world. However, the beneficial effects of stroking a pet dog or cat have now been scientifically proven. This sense of touch and stroking carries powerful messages of love and comfort not only to the animal, but also in return to the person stroking it.

Massage is also increasingly popular, and healing often takes place during a session of massage by a caring practitioner. I use massage and find Abayanga massage particularly beneficial as it rebalances the energy of the body, mind and soul and the chakras, especially when done in a peaceful environment. The whole ritual of massage could be thought of as a Mandala – a container of essence.

Finally there's nothing quite like a hug; you can put your intent into a hug and the recipient can feel it. They know whether it's genuine or not! The quality of a hug is varied; from a quick squeeze to a meaningful embrace. It's all a matter of intention and focus; the Tantric alchemy of transforming energy through awareness.

6. Multi-Sensory Mandalas

Multi-sensory Mandalas can range from solid crystals imbibed with messages, to the more subtle 'ether' that surrounds absolutely everything and affects how we feel in a specific place because of what may have happened there – residual energy [16].

Multi-sensory Mandalas can actually be programmed with intent and in this process we are truly delving into the realms of shamanism and Tantric alchemy, where part of our consciousness is aware of other dimensions of reality.

Once we establish our innate ability for Mandala-making in the five sensory world, we will naturally sense the more subtle energy and discover other realms through our inner connection as we progress.

For some readers this section may be just a step too far for now, yet for others who are already mindful of the subtle energies around us, and some who have perhaps experienced shamanic journeying in the past, it may be a validation of what you already knew you are capable of doing at a deep level – for more see Chapter 8.

So now that we have uncovered the essentials of the Mandala and how it can be used, you may well be inspired to make your own. The next chapter will guide you how to do this as you immerse yourself in the beautiful mystery!

Chapter 4

How To Make Your Own Mandalas

"Practise what you know, and it will help to make clear what now you do not know"
~ Vincent Van Gogh

Learning to work with the Mandala can help us achieve the optimum energy flow that will manifest our intentions through personal experience. If it doesn't work the first time, do it again until it feels 'alive' or 'connected'; until it works for you.

Mandalas act as 'doppelgangers', like extra focused aspects of yourself that help you to increase your energy and in turn increase your ability to manifest, by the power of two or more. With each experience you will learn a little more that you didn't know, you didn't know!

Because art originally stems from our right-brain inspiration rather than from the language-based ego of the logical left-brain, it has the advantage of being non-attached to a logical outcome. This practice offers advantages we have discussed previously, and which become even clearer the more you experience it for yourself.

If this is still a new concept to you, at this point you may feel unconvinced by a promise of being able to effect creation through a drawing, but if you stay open-minded, you might become at least curious enough to have a go and be pleasantly surprised. After all, the Mandala has been around for thousands of years across many if not all cultures, all over the world, used by warriors and by holy men, so therefore it must be worth a little of your time and consideration.

This section will show you how to make Mandalas that I have worked with successfully in the past. Each of them has a different purpose, so choose as is appropriate to your need.

The five types of Mandalas I use are:
1. **Self-enquiry**
2. **Clearing**
3. **Healing**
4. **Manifestation a) subjective or divine b) objective or personal**
5. **Life Line or Future Self**

In order to make Mandalas you'll need paper and a range of colours to draw with.

As you progress you may find you'll want to add to your toolbox. I suggest soft coloured pastels, as they are easy to work with and create lots of movement, which to me can represent energy in the most helpful way. You may get really creative and decide to add coloured papers, fabrics, paints, beads, feathers, crystals, metals, as you proceed... or then again, you may not! ☺

Equipment I suggest for Mandala making:
- Textured cartridge paper pad suitable for use with charcoals and pastels
- A roll of lightly-textured lining paper (wallpaper) cut into A4 or suitable size pieces is great for practising, and works out more cost-effective than a pad of paper – especially for clearing Mandalas.
- A selection of coloured soft pastels, though you can begin with coloured pencils, chalks or crayons if you already have them. Colours that inspire you are best; ideally eight or more colours: red, blue, yellow, green, purple, orange, pink, turquoise, brown, black and white. I much prefer soft pastels to oil pastels, as they flow across the surface of the paper more easily.

- Hair spray or fixative for finished pastel artwork.

1. Self-Enquiry Mandala

This Mandala is a wonderful tool of self-discovery. During a Mandala workshop or retreat, we generally begin and end with a self-enquiry Mandala. By doing this, the participants have tangible evidence of how much their energy has changed throughout the workshop or retreat.

I suggest keeping a file of self-enquiry Mandalas, all dated and filed in order, as a sort of journal of your Mandala making. You can look back on these to see how different things affect your energy and notice if there are cycles; rather like a calendar and map of your journey. You can see how different seasons, different types of food or situations can affect you. It's rather like stopping to take a breath and checking in with how you are feeling in picture form, rather than being limited by words, which sometimes don't tell the truth. As the saying goes, a picture paints a thousand words. In time you will learn to interpret these Mandalas extremely accurately by comparing one to another, it's like learning a new language. Practice is the key.

Whenever you make a Mandala, take the appropriate time to ground yourself back into your normal awareness afterwards, before continuing with everyday life[17].

How To Create A Self-Enquiry Mandala

1. Have your paper and colours to hand. A4 size is good for this, as you can easily file and keep them.
2. Close your eyes and register how you are feeling.
3. Make your intention to draw the energy of how you are feeling.
4. Without thinking about what you are going to draw, simply relax and begin drawing how you feel without trying to draw anything in particular.

5. Allow the drawing to flow from your centre; connect with yourself.

6. If words pop into your mind jot them down and let them go out of your mind again.

7. Get a sense of standing behind yourself looking in at what's happening.

8. Then re-engage and send your awareness around the whole body.

9. Continue until you feel the drawing is complete.

10. Acknowledge that your drawing is a perfect representation of how you feel now in this moment.

2. Clearing Mandala

This Mandala is great for clearing out and letting go of anything that no longer serves you. You have probably heard the saying many times 'let it go', but do you know *how* to let go of feelings, emotions or a negative thought pattern? Well, this is a perfect way to physically and mentally let go. During a Mandala workshop or retreat, we generally do a clearing Mandala just before lunch. By doing this, the participants have the opportunity to take part in the burning ceremony of the Mandala before we eat lunch. I suggest you also do it before eating as the lightness of an empty stomach helps the feeling of being clear and light. Clearing Mandalas can be used to rid yourself of anything at all that feels intrusive to you, either in your body as a virus or illness, in your mind as unhelpful thoughts and perceptions, or in your home as stagnant or uncomfortable energy. You can also add anything unhelpful to your highest good that you don't even know about… that should cover it all!

If you have a major issue, it is more beneficial to focus on this as a separate Mandala so that can get right to the core of it. If you feel you didn't get it all with the first one you can always repeat it until you're happy that it's completely gone.

How To Create A Clearing Mandala

1. Have your paper and colours to hand. Scrap paper is good for this as you are going to burn it anyway.

2. Close your eyes and make your intention to release anything that no longer serves your highest good. If there is something specific you wish to release, intend for that only. Otherwise a general clearing-out of everything that no longer serves you can be intended.

3. Think about the specific thing only; otherwise remember anything that has happened to upset you. It maybe something someone said or something they did. It could be circumstances you feel are beyond your control. In fact anything at all that makes you frightened, angry, hurt, sad, disappointed, stressed or anxious. You get the idea.

4. Without thinking about how you are going to represent these things, just pick a colour that feels right and begin drawing out your emotions. Allow the drawing to flow from your centre. Express the anger and hurt outwardly onto the paper. Get passionate about it; cry or shout if it feels right.

5. If names or words pop into your mind, jot them down and let them go onto the paper without thinking about them over and over – the 90-second rule[18] can be helpful here, although if you feel you need to spend more time on a particularly hurtful issue feel free to follow your intuition.

6. Get a sense of really engaging with what's happening; allow any anguish to be expressed into the drawing. Let it out.

7. When you feel as if the drawing has finished, close your eyes.

8. Acknowledge that your drawing now contains all the unhelpful energies that were previously affecting you from within.

9. Find somewhere safe to burn the drawing – a usable fireplace or else somewhere safe outside. If it's cold outside, put on suitable clothing, as you will definitely want to stay with the

drawing until it is all turned to ash. Watch the flames transform the Mandala and feel it change. Release and breathe out. Watch the colours that may appear in the flames. Take your shoulders up to your ears and then release them. Make tight fists and then release them. Clench your teeth and them release. Finally tighten your buttocks then relax the pelvic floor – this has the extraordinary affect of release. Now acknowledge that you have let go of this baggage. You've cleared out the old energy and you are ready to create a new energy for the future.

3. Healing Mandala

The Healing Mandala is self explanatory – a container for healing energy. Healing Mandalas are made in order to supply healing energy to those that need healing and balancing. I have experienced this personally, and I have witnessed healing done for others through a Mandala, sometimes taking several months to bring healing for a physical condition, and other times bringing instantaneous relief in cases of grief or mental anguish. Shamanic Medicine baskets or pouches are forms of healing Mandalas, the ritual of the Medicine-Man or shaman interacting with herbs, elements, totems, or talismans taken from within the medicine basket to release the energy. Remember, it is the intent behind the ritual that carries the energy. In the same way, by intending a healing Mandala, we become the shaman or healer and we evoke the healing energies that imbue the drawing.

How To Create A Healing Mandala

1. Have your paper and colours to hand.
2. Close your eyes and think of your intention for healing; imagine perfect health. Invite the energy of perfect health into your mind, body and soul. See and feel yourself bathing and relaxing in its energy.

3. Choose colours that intuitively occur to you without thinking about the choice. Simply allow and accept what comes.

4. Without thinking about how you are going to represent the feeling you are having, express the feeling of perfect health onto the paper. You may like to repeat a Mantra of the words 'perfect health' or 'healing energy' as feels right as you draw – or simply send loving and compassionate thoughts to someone you love.

5. Allow yourself to picture images that represent perfect health; maybe yourself enjoying perfect health, fit athletes or even luscious green plants you may have seen. Perhaps use imagery of clear fresh water, a blue sky, or sunshine anything at all that evokes the idea of vibrant healthy energy. If possible, remember a time when you felt full of energy directly after exercise or a lovely walk in nature. Evoke the glowing tingly feeling of the body responding to the memories of these activities.

6. Do not try to draw what you see; instead use the imagery to affect your own energy. Relax and feel it, drawing without trying to control.

7. Get a sense of really engaging with what's happening; allow nurturing feelings to be expressed in the drawing. Pause and experience your body relaxing into this nurturing energy, and use several pauses as part of the practise.

8. If you should find your attention wandering, simply stop drawing and bring your focus back to your intention before you continue. Relax into it again.

9. If ever there is a sense of attachment to the outcome for someone close to you stop drawing and relax. Reconnect by imagining perfect health again before you draw any more. Have trust the Mandala will work, as fear and doubt will block the energy; it needs to be clear and light.

10. When you feel the drawing has finished close your eyes.

11. Acknowledge that your drawing contains all the powerful

energies of healing and balancing – that everything you associate with perfect health is stored within your drawing.

12. Relax more, and enjoy what you have just created!

13. Feel free to share your Mandala with those in need.

14. Remember, it is powerful to place a glass of water on the Mandala for twenty minutes or so. The water absorbs the healing vibrations and may be enjoyed.

4. Manifestation Mandala

Manifestation Mandalas are used to manifest either objective or subjective intentions for collective and personal benefit. As your awareness of energy increases, it is possible to create Mandalas that can evoke very powerful results for all who perceive them, and especially those operating on the unconscious and subconscious levels. Mandalas can be developed for subjective inner purposes, such as to promote healing, focus, upliftment, and joy, or for objective outer manifestations – from a new pair of shoes to a new home.

When we begin to formulate and contemplate the ideas of what we would like to manifest, we often become clearer about what we don't want. It's often easier to decide the things we don't want, rather than what we want. However, knowing what we don't want often allows us, by a process of elimination, to discover what we do want... eventually.

This preparation time is the most important stage of this process. Often in workshops and on retreat we spend the longest amount of time focused on deciding what it is that we want to manifest. It goes through a process of change, because often we won't allow ourselves to ask for what we really want; instead we ask for what we think we *should* want, or what would sound best. Most people eventually do get down to what they really want in the end, and they are often inspired by sharing their ideas with the group. Working from home without the benefit of listening to other people's ideas can be more challenging, so you may like to involve a friend, even if it's chatting by phone. In my experience, bouncing ideas around leads to very worthwhile intentions!

Once your intention is decided, the experience of single-point focus meditation will help you to create more potent drawings, and it is worth investing some time practising this before you even start to make a Mandala. You can simply pick two contrasting subjects to think about. Perhaps one could be trees, and the other your career – or something that you are planning to do. Then alternate your thoughts between them; first think about the tree for a whole minute, then switch and think about your project, for a minute. Keep switching, and do not allow yourself to go back to the previous subject – no matter how interesting and seductive it may have become. Discipline your thoughts to follow your direction. This is a great exercise to do if you are on a train or a bus, changing subject at each stop so you don't have to time yourself. Continue for around 10 to 15 minutes, or longer if you enjoy it.

It can also help you to fine tune your purpose or intent. People who are good at focusing their mind and who meditate regularly will find making the Mandala easier. But even if you don't meditate, you can still create a Mandala; that's the whole point of using art in this way. That said, the Mandala's energy will reflect the strength, clarity and focused intention of its creator, so practice pays off.

The clearer and more focused you are, even if it is only in short bursts, the more your Mandala will manifest. A Mandala may take several sittings to complete, and it can develop and intensify as your energy settles and your logical mind lets go to the flow. Each one is alive with its own intent.

How To Create A Manifesting Mandala

1. Have your paper and colours to hand. You may like to play some relaxing music or use Tracks 6 and 7 of my companion

CD *The Art Of Being ...Psychic,* which are produced to trigger right-brain awareness.

2. Set your intention and contemplate it for as long as is comfortable.

3. Once you are settled in mind and body, focus on the colours you feel are helpful for your purpose, and have them to hand.

4. Without thinking about how you are going to represent the intention, simply focus on that intention as you begin to draw onto the paper. You may like to repeat a Mantra of the words that express your intention as you draw.

5. Let the drawing flow as it connects you to the OM – as if it has a life of its own. I sometimes become inspired to use shapes, words or symbols as the basis for a manifestation Mandala, and other times I just don't know what will evolve. Simply allow the connection without thinking or trying.

6. Continue to draw focusing only on your intention, as well as how you'll feel as you ultimately achieve your goal. Stop drawing if you become distracted with other thoughts, or if you feel annoyed, or you notice the energy falls away. Wait until the energy connection returns before you continue drawing.

7. Producing a manifestation Mandala can take a long time, or it can be finished very quickly. Each Mandala is different, as each has a different purpose. Mandalas should be allowed to emerge with effortless effort, enjoyment and creativity. Leave any judgement to one side, and simply allow them to become as they are.

8. Look at the Mandala and let yourself feel its energy. There should be a feeling that it is 'alive', and if you cannot connect with that feeling, its best to start the whole thing again until you can.

Your completed Mandala will be alive with the intention you make at the onset. When you contemplate the drawing, you may notice elements in it that you didn't see at the time of creating it, which confirms you were in right-brain activity. This is always a good sign. Accept these elements, even if at first you don't know what they represent. Through contemplation the answer will come; often this is delivered in surprising ways.

5. Life-Plan or Future-Self Mandala

These Mandalas can be more intense because they are ongoing, and a certain amount of previous experience in Mandala-making and or guidance from an experienced person is an advantage. These projects can develop and change over several years and act to guide your life intentions rather than one-off specific goals or qualities. They are like a map that you can change, should your pathway become unfavourable. It's like having another 'you' to hold your hand and remind you to be balanced and focused. I always advise doing a clearing Mandala first so that you can begin with a clean slate.

How to make a Life-Plan Mandala

The basic technique is the same as for the manifestation Mandala given previously, but the premise is that the empty page or canvas is worked on using the principles of Feng Shui placement to guide where certain aspects of your life need to be drawn. Once again see Fig 2 for the Feng Shui map of your home.

When what you have drawn causes a noticeable result, you can monitor it and fine-tune it – even change it as necessary. This applies to all areas of your life. It is good to focus on one section at a time, and using your intuition you will know when to draw on different areas and when to leave them be for a while. Below are guidance notes for the different areas, and the type of intentions that may work best there. Sometimes more than one area will seem appropriate, and they will link together in a natural blend: let intuition be your guide; know that you know best for you!

Guidance Notes (and these not set in stone!)

Draw in your **Wealth** corner; top left hand corner of the page, when:

- You want to gain abundance
- You want to increase what you can manifest
- You want to feel wealthy to attract wealth
- You are going to ask for a pay-rise

Draw in your **Admiration** area; top middle of page, when:

- You want to improve your reputation
- You need to summon up the courage to do something new
- You want to become admired for something and get the credit you deserve

Draw in your **Relationship** area; top right hand corner, when:

- You want a more positive interaction with people
- You are looking for a loving relationship
- You want to make a good connection between you and another person.
- You are thinking of settling down in a relationship (marriage or living together)
- You want to put sparkle back into an old relationship

Draw on the **Family** and **Stability** area; left mid page:

- When you want to improve family relationships
- When you feel you need to increase security
- When you need to trust yourself to do the right thing
- To increase self-worth

Draw on the **Children** and **Creativity** area; right mid page:

- To conceive a child
- To help your children
- When you need to be more creative
- For rejuvenation

- When you are starting a new venture
- To increase your own creativity

Draw on the **Skill** and **Wisdom** area; bottom left corner:
- To gain wisdom
- For help in passing an exam
- For clear decisions
- To improve skills

Draw on the **Career** and **Life Path** area; bottom centre:
- To get employment
- To change employment
- To clarify your life purpose
- To improve your business
- To increase your income

Draw on the **Travel** and **Helpful People** area; bottom right corner when:
- Moving home
- Travelling
- You need help with something
- You want to connect with the Zeitgeist – spirit of the times

Draw on the **Health** area; right in the centre of the page when:
- You want overall better health
- You want to increase vitality
- You want to shake off an imbalance in your system
- To improve a situation that just doesn't fit anywhere else

Well, by now I trust you are inspired or even just curious enough to start creating your own Mandalas. Should you need a little more guidance, come along and do a workshop or retreat with me[19].

Chapter 5

Mandala and You – Co-Creation

"An audience or 'viewer' is necessary to create a Mandala.
Where there is no you, there is no Mandala"
~ Longchen Rabjampa

Once we have created a Mandala, it is essential that we interact with it. Communication is a two-way flow. The intention embedded into the artwork goes into our perception on different levels of awareness, and affects us on each level. Some students have complained to me that their Mandalas have not worked; they sometimes get very upset wondering why it works for others but not for them. I find, on questioning them, that their Mandala is rolled up in a drawer or somewhere out of sight – of course it didn't work; you didn't interact with it. By rolling it up and putting it in a drawer, you closed the doorway on your intention and your connection, literally cutting it off!

This attitude of 'my Mandala doesn't work' is similar to the belief that whatever happens to us, especially the bad stuff, happens 'out there' and is someone else's fault – this can cause anger, resentment and disempowerment (fear). Some of us even credit the good stuff that happens in our lives to something 'out there' such as fate, karma, destiny or God. This gives in to fear, and makes it challenging to get a sense that we have any possibility to create the things we need within the Divine Plan.

So here's the thing: the truth is that we do have possibility to create all that we need, and this form of shamanic and Tantric Art is re-emerging as a very significant and important tool for us right now at this time.

Using the Mandala is central to help us realise that we are definitely co-creators. That we can; in fact we MUST, TAKE RESPONSIBILITY for creating our lives, our world, and our reality. Through the simple act of realisation, we become empowered to do this with awareness. The 'magic' begins in our mind and ignites what is; what we are. We are powerful, we are capable, and we are just *beginning* to get it!

The strength of the Mandala is that we play our part in the interaction; in the connection; and without us, there is no Mandala. It works best when it's on display – where it can act as a constant reminder of our intentions. The mind is so often dragged off course due to the circumstances we put ourselves under that we need to be reminded of our intentions so we can create the life we are inspired to create.

If we are honest with ourselves, how often do we plan something and then reach the end of the day or week disappointed, to find that we haven't completed that goal? When we sit down to think about something, we find that we have drifted into thinking about something else totally unrelated? The 'Rambling Mind' can be especially upsetting at night, when we are tired or exhausted, and really want to sleep. Thoughts and ideas crop up to get our attention, each one convincing us they are so very important that we must think about them right now, however tired we may be!

Learning to create Mandalas will help in this situation. The creation phase is a very empowering experience, and a helpful way to practise controlling your mind. Once the mind is focused it becomes very powerful. You are very powerful! A mind that is working in cooperation, rather than competition, is far more helpful. The art of manifesting your intentions easily becomes within your domain, and on top of that, you can create a good nights' sleep!

As well as a way to focus your mind on your goal, the Mandala is used as a re-mind-er to shift your frequency, to a vibration that can attract that specific goal. It acts as a subtle force-field of energy that sends its message to the subconscious, unconscious, and the conscious mind. Mandala communicates with your total being, not just single moments of awareness. The only way to really understand and feel this is to experience the connection yourself.

Using either visual or audible Mandalas – and sometimes both – I have helped many people to manifest their intentions. This is a tool that works, not just for one person – the shaman – as was the case historically, but for all people who are prepared to invest a little time throwing off their inhibitions in order to develop their own creative potential. We are all potentially artists and shamans. Shamans have helpers in all dimensions. Mandalas can be these helpers.

People sometimes ask me if it's best to focus on one Mandala at a time – and I usually say yes. In my experience, especially when we are just beginning, it helps to make a Mandala, focus on it, and then experience it working in our lives before diluting our attention by making more.

The following stories are about different people who have embraced Mandalas and had objective results. They share these experiences in order to help others believe that the process works, in order that you will be inspired to invest the time to become the maker of your reality. I would like to take this opportunity to thank them all.

One very common situation is that someone is so busy in their lives that they forget to acknowledge when their Mandala has worked for them, and sometimes lose the power given by acknowledgement. Joanne was such a case...

Joanne's story – The Forgotten Mandala

Joanne joined us for a workshop in the summer of 2007. She made a Mandala for a new home, and this would also affect various difficult aspects of her life related to that move. Joanne tells her story...

About a year ago I went on June-Elleni's weekend workshop in Somerset. It was a magical time of exploring colour and art including Mandala making. This was fascinating as she explained that Mandalas could manifest the dream or desire that one intends at that moment in time.

I was going through a very traumatic relationship break-up and had to look for a place to live and work. It was a daunting task, as I had to try and sell a rented flat I owned and then find a suitable abode. I imagined all the problems associated with doing it and wondered how it was going to happen – especially the financial aspect. So this seemed like a good time to manifest my new home with the Mandala.

I drew a beautiful picture with the central area being a deep pink heart. While I drew, I thought with great joy of my new home and how I would feel inside it. Then, I put the Mandala on the wall to look at throughout the day.

Time passed, and I was very busy thinking about property. Suddenly in the space of a month, I sold my studio flat to a good buyer and then almost immediately found a new, cosy, perfect little terrace. It had a room to work from with a downstairs toilet; just perfect for clients. It was in one of my favorite areas; one that I thought I could not afford, near the sea and my favourite walks. It all went so smoothly I was amazed. Not one glitch.

I had pretty much forgotten about my Mandala. It was still on the wall and I automatically pass it daily, but didn't think about it. Then out the blue I spoke to Ian Dale, and he asked how the house-hunting was going. I told him I had a lovely little house. He then said "Well, that Mandala worked then". I stopped in amazement as I had forgotten about it and told him so.

Later that day I started thinking, and realised the enormity of what had happened – and how the Mandala that I looked at daily had indeed played a major part in helping everything come together to get the house of my dreams. And how easily it can happen that we can side-step it and almost forget about it in the day-to-day business of living. I felt quite ashamed of myself, and took the Mandala down and had a chat to it and looked at the colours and the large pink heart, and realised I was living the heart in the house as I was so happy and my heart every day is filled with so much love.

So for me not only was the drawing of the house Mandala a life-changing experience, but also a lesson in how a Mandala can help us manifest anything that is for our highest good created with our best intentions. And that we should honour Mandalas, believing and knowing what we intend through them can and will come to pass. I learnt that they are a very powerful request to the universe, which can manifest in truly remarkable ways.

Joanne Figov - Bowen Complementary therapist

Eva's Story – Positive Interactions Mandala Cures Dog Phobia

Eva's phobia started with the unhelpful experience in childhood of her grandparent's dog tied up outside – a guard-dog rather than a pet – who was therefore encouraged to bark and growl if anyone approached. The dog did its job very well indeed, and in the process of his work managed to terrify Eva as a little girl.

Even as an adult Eva panicked at the thought of coming close to a dog, and made sure that wherever she went, there were no dogs... and if there were, she simply chose not to go! Until the day she came to my workshop, somehow she had booked this workshop without making her regular enquiry, "Do you have a dog?" So unknown to Eva, she was about to set foot outside her comfort zone in more ways than one!

Eva arrived early and pulled into the car park, just as another participant was arriving at the venue. Jodie ran happily wagging her tail to meet the cars, much to Eva's dismay. Jodie is a black and white collie dog, and a very friendly one at that! Eva froze. The other participant approached Jodie and patted her, much to her delight. Looking around to see why Eva wasn't getting out of her car, Joanne approached Eva's car to find out why. We then had to lock Jodie in the house so that a very unhappy Eva could venture in.

By lunchtime, Eva had settled into the workshop and had begun to make her Mandala. She decided to create positive interactions with other beings. She seemed happy and relaxed at this point, and so I had forgotten about her phobia. However unnoticed by me everyone else moved through into the food area for lunch except Eva. I was busily offering food to everyone when I suddenly realised there was one missing. Eva was not there. Jodie came running through wagging her tail and trying to get my attention. I followed her; she led me to the workshop room where I saw Eva peeping through the window of the closed door very distressed. I knew then that Jodie had come to get me. Later Eva told me she had sent a telepathic message to Jodie to come and get me! Was the positive interaction Mandala working already, I wondered?

Once the afternoon session was complete, Eva had finished her Mandala and felt confident about it, so we decided to put it to the test. We were inspired to ask Eva if she would like to meet Jodie with all of us close by to support her and, astonishingly, she agreed. Amazing really, considering she had never been able to go near a dog in her life! Slowly Eva approached Jodie, who laid flat on the floor because she sensed Eva's anxiety; and within 20 minutes Eva was feeding Jodie biscuits!

The Mandala had reflected Eva's intention to make positive interactions, even though her interaction with Jodie was something she could not have imagined. But for Eva the best part of the story was yet to come... Eva's daughter was expecting her first baby, but Eva had already decided she would probably not go to see her grandchild as they'd recently bought a dog. A painful decision, but understandable; fear is a terrible thing. So because of Salty, Eva believed she must wait perhaps several years before meeting her grandchild. Imagine the joy Eva felt as she held the baby in her arms only a few days after the birth, with Salty sitting next to them on the sofa, watching and wagging his tail!

Jackie's Story – Mandala in the drawer

Jackie decided she had enough of living out of boxes and suitcases. She wanted a home of her own and she wanted it now! Problem was she couldn't find anything she liked in a location that was suitable and convenient for work. A year had passed without seeing anything worthy of an offer, and she was becoming more and more upset. The more upset she was, the less she felt like looking at property, and so it went on – a vicious circle of feeling down about the situation of living in a temporary place that she disliked.

Jackie told me about the problem and we decided that she would make a Mandala to create the property of her dreams. I suggested that rather than trying to draw a picture of what she wanted, she should focus on how it would feel. To imagine a warm and homely feeling connected with the house. I advised that she choose colours that would evoke this feeling, and as she drew to put every single thought of her perfect home into the drawing – without trying to make the drawing into anything specific, rather just allowing it to form organically. It was done and on reflection it made Jackie smile by just looking at the image… a good sign I thought.

Several months later I had a phone call from Jackie: "My Mandala isn't working," she said indignantly, "and I really believed it would. So what can I do now?"

"Where is your Mandala?" I asked.

"Rolled up safely in my drawer at home." She replied

"That's why it isn't working then…. put it on the wall, you are supposed to interact with it to make it work."

"Ah ha, I forgot that bit, okay, will do."

Three weeks later a home was found, and an excited Jackie

called again: "I found it, I love it, I put on an offer and they accepted it! What shall I do now?"

"How about you move in."

<laughter>

Jackie is now happily living in her dream home.

Ian's Story – A challenging house to sell

Ian's house had been on the market a little over two years, mostly because it was the type of property that required a very specific buyer. The house had been extended to accommodate a recording studio and offices, so it wasn't just a residence; there was a business involvement as well. Ian tells his story:

Working with June on Mandala workshops I am always amazed at their power and success. It is very rewarding to hear the many success stories after workshops. So with the desire to create a new home I set to work on my own Mandala. My intention was to sell the property where I lived and worked in order to manifest a new family home. The property we were living in was large and unusual and having tried to sell it over a two-year period, buyers were not forthcoming.

As I began, I found myself thinking about what my picture was going to look like – an obvious image came to mind of a square building with windows, a chimney (with smoke), a path leading to a door in the middle, a tree in the garden (which had a picket fence) and sun in the sky! I knew this wasn't helpful, and that I needed to clear my mind to allow an inspired image to appear on the canvas based on my feelings and not my thoughts. When I let go and the Mandala took shape, to my amazement I found myself creating a picture of a blue sea and a sun rising or setting on the horizon, which reflected bright orange in the blue.

When it was complete I was discussing the outcome with June and we agreed that the Mandala was showing the emotions I needed to acknowledge regarding the sale of a family home we had lived in for many years.

I put the Mandala on the wall in my office/house and looked at it daily. Within a couple of weeks we had an offer from a potential buyer. How great! I was very happy and soon after I took the Mandala down as we began to pack our things... hmm, was it a coincidence that the newly-found buyers decided the house was not right for them? So, I put the Mandala back up and again new buyers were soon putting an offer on the house. This time the Mandala stayed there until the day we moved out! It may be worth mentioning that we found a house to buy, and completed on the day before we moved out. In this case the Universe reflected the intention on my Mandala perfectly.

In summary my advice would be:
- Have no perception of what you are about to draw
- Make sure you put the Mandala somewhere you can see it
- Allow the process to complete
- Acknowledge its success

Ian Dale – Music publisher and Satvik Sound Healer

Mark's Story – A Radio Show or two!
Mark's story is short and sweet, and one I will always remember as it worked for me as well! Mark made his Mandala when we were on retreat in Somerset. He decided that he wanted to host a radio show, and that it would be a good idea to make a Mandala to manifest this show.

I remember spending quite a bit of time looking at Mark's Mandala. I was very drawn to it and didn't fully realise it at the time. The day after the retreat I was offered a radio show, and three weeks later Mark got his show too. The power of two or more!

Max's Story – Uncomfortable Energy in the Office
I felt that the energy in Max's office needed to be transformed, so

when I had printed the first few Mandalas I had created, I gave them to him even before I had finished the complete range. His story is the first feedback I was given from the Mandalas I made.

Max tells his story:

As a psychotherapist, I am fascinated by the work of Carl Jung, and was surprised to learn that he did a Mandala drawing every day for a number of years. Jung evidently considered the Mandala to be a powerful representation of the unconscious self, and so I was thrilled to experiment with the use of Mandala drawings in my own life.

In one of my roles, I spend a lot of time in a central London office, which has been, for decades, the epicentre of some rather tricky and difficult conversations on behalf of an established educational establishment. It became apparent to me and to many who entered the office that the atmosphere wasn't what it ought to be; it was described as 'sticky', 'sharp', 'fractious' and so on.

All I knew was that it was difficult for me to settle down in what is, architecturally at least, a grand and beautiful space – and it seemed to be equally uncomfortable for many visitors. With June -Elleni's help, I displayed a quartet of Mandalas depicting and delineating four words that could be said to belong to the 'collective unconscious'. I thought it would be nice to frame them, displaying them behind my desk. And then I said nothing, but waited.

Wow! The reaction, and the feedback from others, took a turn from what I expected. I was anticipating a few, "Nice images, Max", as feedback, but I got less of that and more of, "There's something different about this room." People started staying longer, the quality of our conversations seemed to have more depth and openness, and the space didn't make me feel so tired or uncomfortable.

Nobody could seem to put it into words, but there was definitely a consistent trend. So I collaborated with June-Elleni to place another quartet of Mandalas in my south London workspace. It was the same: people felt more relaxed, I seemed more productive, and I seemed less 'urgent' and fidgety. The power of focus that for some time had eluded me appeared to come back in spates.

I can't seem to put it into words except to borrow from the words of Jung: perhaps the Mandala is indeed a representation of the unconscious self. What I do know is that it's a powerful tool and a statement of intent, one which I would not want to be without.

Max Eames
Psychotherapist and author of Wealth Mechanic

Jeannie's Story – Mandala in the garage

Jeannie has many years' experience of how energy works, and so she was very curious when I first began to talk to her about my work with Mandalas. As an artist, she was inspired to have a go, so when the opportunity arose to create one for selling her house, along with other techniques she already had in her repertoire, she embraced the idea immediately. I just love how she placed the Mandala in the garage, an empty space with nothing much to see accept the Mandala – and all potential buyers want to pop their nose into the garage, even briefly, don't they? When they did, there it was working its magic!

Jeannie tells her story:

In October 2007, I was selling my house amid the unfolding crisis of Northern Rock, which was creating a nervous tension among buyers. In the preceding months, I had already focused on several energetic levels to prepare my house for selling. On the physical level, I had redecorated all the rooms using a neutral soft linen paint throughout, and had de-cluttered and put most of my personal effects into storage in order to present a fresh, spacious feel to attract buyers.

On the Devic level, I had called in the help of the Nature Spirits and the garden was lush and colourful, despite it being autumn when most plants should have been turning inwards for their winter rest. I had used crystals to complete the Feng Shui balance of the house, and I had laid an energy trail from the front door of the estate agents to my own front door, to pull buyers in.

The house was now ready to go on the market amid daily news bulletins of doom and gloom in the property market. Then June-Elleni told me about the power of Mandalas and suggested that I make one for the house to reflect joy to everyone who came to view it. "It will make them respond positively," she said. So I chose some pastels in soft blue, pink and yellow hues, which suggested joy to me, and working with a traditional circular format, I started to play with the crayons, not knowing quite what I was doing or how it would look. Smudging, rubbing, adding more colours; slowly a vibrant starburst emerged.

Then I wondered where to put it. Having just decorated my house, it didn't feel right to just pin it on the wall, so I wandered round the house, then decided to sit it on the shelf in the garage/workroom, facing the door, so that everyone who opened the garage door would immediately see it. And if they didn't actually notice it, I knew the energy would be there for them to respond to on an unconscious level.

Viewings began, and within a fortnight four people said they wanted the house. One buyer proceeded straight away and, despite the wobbles in the property market, it was the easiest completion I have ever known. The estate agent said it was "the dream sale".

So was it the Mandala that achieved the ideal outcome, or was it a combination of all the above? I don't know, but I do feel that the Mandala was a powerful aspect of everything I did, and I will certainly explore using more Mandalas in the future.

Jeannie Kar – Artist, Life Coach and Spiritual Counsellor

Sarla's Story – Healing Mandala

Sarla had trigger thumb – that is when the thumb becomes stuck caused by thickening of the tendon or sheath, which prevents the normal smooth movement of the tendon inside the sheath. Sometimes it can be treated with injections, but mostly surgery is needed to free it up successfully. Sarla didn't want either surgery or injections, so she decided to make a Mandala to heal it for herself. Because she is already a qualified healer based at London's College Of Psychic Studies, she put some of her healing know-how into the picture as she drew, and it certainly had a beneficial energy.

After making the Mandala during a workshop, I didn't see Sarla for a couple of months. When she next turned up to do a course with me, she was smiling and delighted to show me her hand. The thumb had regained perfect movement again, truly a powerful healing!

Chapter 6

Meet Me In The Field

"Out beyond ideas of wrongdoing and right doing, there is a field. I'll meet you there"
~ Rumi

What or where is the field out beyond ideas of what is right and wrong? A cornfield perhaps containing intricate crop circles, maybe, but probably not. Fractals then, they contain fields or patterns that seem to bring order to apparent chaos. They show the art of formation and expansion; these successful patterns that nature repeats over and over, to manifest microcosm to macrocosm. Maybe, but still maybe not, even the creative principal of fractals is not out beyond the ideas of doing. So where then, is this field that stands outside creation?

Could it be the field of consciousness in which we all exist? A field that Rumi implies, we can only 'meet' in when we forego judgement of right and wrong, where we must 'be' and not 'do'. In other words, when we are 'out' of our minds; when we enter our right-brain hemisphere and shut out our judgmental ego.

I believe it is here, omni-present and yet beyond; filled with possibility and energy, and at the same time spacious and boundless.

Within this boundless energy-field of pure potential, Mandalas are able to work on three levels of our awareness: **conscious, sub-conscious** and **unconscious** – Depending on which level we operate on, this will affect our ability to understand how the Mandala is affecting us in our field of awareness in any moment. However, let's be clear, the Mandala still affects us, regardless of our ability to understand or even perceive its energy. It works on the energy-field that surrounds and connects all things together, the field where we unconsciously meet together in the Oneness.

If we are reacting **unconsciously** – our ability is latent – we are only aware of an individual instinct for creating our basic survival needs. Here we are oblivious to our full potential, also unaware that we are unaware, and looking outward into the physical world for reasons why things happen to us, and for somebody else to blame. Mostly we criticise and complain about what others are doing, unaware that we are receiving from them what we project out. If we could stop to take notice of Mandalas in the first place, we may 'hope' they will work and bring us what we wish for, but we don't really believe that they can. Or we judge those who use them to be naïve or superstitious. The Mandala however, will still affect us in a very powerful way, even though we are unaware that it is having such an effect. We may under-stand this simply at the level in which someone created a pleasing picture, and we feel good when we look at it. This 'feeling good' is how we respond to the unconscious connection.

If we are reacting at the **Sub-conscious** level – our ability is sporadic – we are present but not fully aware. Here we are intuitively aware of our full potential as creators, but consciously give power away to a separate 'Creator' or 'God' that we can't see, and whom we believe represents the real reason why things happen to us. We may no longer criticise others, but could feel as if we are much more aware than we really are. When we see the Mandala has worked for other people, we start to believe it could work for us as well. We unite with the group sub-conscious, where various thought-forms are 'acted out' in other dimensions, which may appear in our dreams.

The Mandala works at this level by forming a pattern or mould which affects our behaviour in the physical dimension; after interacting with it we are compelled to take a course of action without knowing why. We may recognise this guidance at certain times, but we can also go into denial if something we judge to be 'bad' happens to us before we receive the intended result. We feel a connection sometimes and not at others, which may cause mood swings. The subconscious has a powerful effect, without us knowing how or why.

When we are **Conscious** – we are powerfully intentional – we are completely awake to our union with the Omniversal Consciousness, and know our response to the divine plan. We are aware that we are aware, and we encourage others to join in conscious co-creation, to 'be' the reason why things happen.

At this stage our body expands its energy field and in turn our awareness is expanded. We become aware of Divine Will, and are able to trust the power of manifestation anchored through our will, whatever the outcome. We are non-attached, and we become the Mandala as we create and blend with it.

Here we are fully aware of our potential to co-create our reality and can consciously move through alternative dimensions as necessary to do so. We simply know that we are always connected, even when things seem to go 'wrong.'

Mandalas work on subtle as well as tangible levels. They are subtle like homeopathy, and to some extent they are more physical like a talisman. Because of their range, they are very powerful. The spiritual energy communicates directly to the soul – the intentional energy to the mind and the physical energy to the manifest universe – so they can affect us completely and wholly. They are valuable tools to help our awareness expand, and for us to take control of our mind.

The most powerful and helpful use of a Mandala, in my opinion, is to promote universal values and qualities within us, such as peace, happiness, joy and eventually enlightenment. These are more valuable that material wealth because, once achieved, they can never be lost or stolen, and will continue to attract and manifest the energy of everything that is appropriate to the highest good. All that you need; although not always all that your ego thinks you want!

Mandalas reflect the strength, clarity and focused intention of their creators. Naturally the clearer and more focused we become, the more potent our Mandalas will be. It's a very simple truth, and highlights the importance of taking personal responsibility. Remember, Mandala making is a powerful tool, and should not be taken lightly or abused. If used with a reverence for life, respecting the free will of others, it will serve its maker very well. If it is used for personal gain or by attempting to affect others against their will, be prepared for the karmic consequences.

I have now come to think of this type of art as a physical representation of prayer and even as an expression of divinity, to represent future, and as a tool for co-creation as well as prediction; a way to multiply our intent, even as a friend or twin soul to help us grow. This concept is cemented by various personal and shared experiences; firstly with Precognitive Art – during my career as a fashion designer – through my interest in science and the brain, and finally through shamanic, tantric or psychic art.

We seem to be moving away from the word 'psychic' in search of a new label for a different paradigm, one that frees us from the image of a gypsy fortune-teller.

As science and parapsychology investigates this idea of sensing beyond logic, we find, without doubt, our ability to interact with the fields of energy that surrounds us. We feel this ability more strongly the more our awareness grows; and I consider that the way we can interact with it is the key now. During this interaction, we discover abilities that are far beyond what we normally expect; from remote viewing to telepathy, from healing to finding a hidden physical strength beyond our normal capacity. Sometimes we fall upon these abilities seemingly by accident, and often only recognise them by looking back at the experience after the event. One thing, though, is certain: most people I speak to have had some kind of experience of this connection, even though some have never acknowledged it before I asked!

I believe we are constantly interacting with the unseen energy fields that surround us. Quantum Field Interaction (QFI) could accurately label this extra-sensory ability we all have, which has been called psychic, and thought of by many as a mysterious hoax. Unfortunately, the idea of psychic ability as a hoax was brought about by people who exaggerate and cheat, and there are some of those in every profession. But it's not a hoax; it has just been misunderstood, and now we are getting closer to under-standing more clearly how normal it is. If a simple name change can bring a more serious attitude forward, I am all for that.

Science acknowledges that we do not fully understand why energy at the quantum level acts differently from what is experi-enced in the larger world. And this is a very exciting time to be alive. These quantum fields of energy are where Einstein's 'spooky action at a distance' occurs, when there appears to be a transfer of information from one particle to another faster than the speed of light.

If it can happen on a tiny scale, why not in the world at large? And maybe this is where we need to look more closely at fractals. Fractals are not just complex shapes and pretty pictures generated by computers. Anything that, on the surface, appears random and irregular could be a fractal. They saturate our lives, appearing as tiny membranes of a cell and as huge constellations in the solar system. Fractals are unique, irregular patterns left behind by possible movements of the chaotic world in action. In theory, we could say everything in this world has a fractal nature: fern leaves, mould growth, veins in a body, branches of tracheal tubes, water swirling and spiralling from a spout, cumulus clouds, DNA molecules, snowflakes, crystal formation and growth, patterns of migrating animals, population spread, and even the stock market fluctuations!

Scientists, mathematicians and artists are excited by fractals, and have utilised them in their studies for centuries. They are associated with Chaos Theory, suggesting there are patterns within chaos, and although they depict chaotic behaviour, when we look carefully, we can uncover repetitions within the design of creation.

To some, the study of chaos and fractals is more than just a new field in science that unifies mathematics, theoretical physics, art and computer science. As described in Jude Currivan's books *The Wave* and *CosMos – a creator's guide to the whole-world* (co-authored with Ervin Laszlo) it heralds a transformation in our consciousness and our understanding of who we really are.

The discovery of a new language, and one that is able to describe the infinite universe we live in; one of continuous motion and not static images; suggests plasticity rather than rules that are set in stone; perhaps natures' own animated artwork.

Today, scientists are experimenting with applications for fractal mathematics, which can make predictions on everything from stock-market prices to weather and climate changes. We will see how this develops over time, no doubt, and what if any association it has with anomalous precognition and or QFI!

Fractals have great potential because they can describe the real world better than traditional mathematics and physics. They seem to mirror nature and how it follows patterns of the simplest and most efficient path of formation. Not only flat, but also expanding out through dimensions. Unexplainable, seemingly complicated, yet tantalisingly simple and very close to clarification. Perhaps this is nature's messenger, using art to contain the mystery of life, the Unified Theory; the big TOE! – Theory Of Everything!

A host of exciting experiments beyond the normal five senses is now being brought to light by scientists, as mentioned in Appendix 1, and many others besides, as well as professors in a growing number of UK and US universities. Also through journalists such as Lynne McTaggert using her coverage of the 'intention experiment' to show how we can affect reality through intent.

The point I am making is simply that if most people we speak to have experienced something, from such a wide variety of lifestyles including scientists, artists and journalists; we simply have to consider that there could be some truth in it, and indeed consider what it could mean to each of us.

If only some of it is true, in an agreement-based reality, the truth is plural. It appears we do live in an agreement-based reality, where if a critical mass of people all agree the same thing, no matter how ridiculous it may sound to previous generations, it becomes true through co-creation!

We all add to the creative melting pot; each and every one of us is part of the bigger picture. Maybe we're each like a small piece of the jigsaw puzzle; or small set of fractals; a necessary small part of the complete whole. When we think about our fascination for jigsaw puzzles, maybe this holds a clue. Why do we enjoy them so much? We seek to separate the pieces of a picture, only to bring them back together to see the picture complete again... sometimes becoming obsessive, especially if we find a piece is missing! An interesting process and a powerful metaphor indeed!

Chapter 7

Artist? Scientist? Shaman?

"Where spirit does not work with the hand, there is no art"
~ Leonardo DaVinci

How can a man who lived in the 1400s have created workable drawings of helicopters and diving equipment, just to mention but two of his extraordinary inventions? Leonardo DaVinci was in my opinion interacting with the Quantum Energy Field in a way that few could interact with it; in a way that an artist does with their right-brain hemisphere. His quote implies knowledge of spirit working with his hand. Perhaps the energy of his era, the Renaissance – an age of re-birth and revival – was the catalyst that enabled his awareness of this interaction; perhaps he was simply tuned in ahead of his time.

We cannot know the answers to these thought-provoking questions, but what we can see, is that this dynamic interaction is happening again now, and it's happening to more than one person. In fact it's happening to many of us, and it's probably happening to you! Maybe you're aware of it; maybe you're not sure. But what you probably sense is that something feels quite different to the way it did…as little as five years ago, and if you are sensitive and aware, maybe even just about a year ago.

So how will we survive this age in which we are living; the changing energy is coming in so much faster now; how can we best cope with what's happening? Looking back on our history may hold some answers that will help us move forwards, with a little more savvy. Traditional paths followed with an open heart and mind can lead beyond boundaries once rigid, to exciting new territory!

The late Ian Xen Lungold, an artist, gave inspired lectures sharing his interpretation of the ancient Mayan calendar [20], expressing his belief that art is a shaman's tool of manifestation, rather than simply decoration. A prayer, if you will, to create what the artist wished to happen; primordial alchemy! He deduced that art first showing up approximately 40,000 years ago during the 'fifth-day' period in the Cultural Cycle (which is also the fifth cycle on the Mayan calendar) must be significant.

"Art was very, very important," he said, "because art was the consciousness of future; it was the first expression of future."

Working in association with Dr Carl J. Calleman, Ian Xen Lungold brings to light the significance of this 'fifth-day' period, by looking back over the previous cycles, to find breakthroughs of great significance occurring repeatedly in each of the fifth-day periods in every cycle. For example, consider the evidence of first organic life on the planet, that life moved onto the land, that fire was used by mankind, that art was found in caves, through to more recent events like, Christ teaching that we are all divine, Einstein publishing E = MC2; all momentous events!

In the course of Ian Xen-Lungold's research, he collated powerful examples like these, which give us the sense that evolution is 'on a schedule'. And, that each of these 'fifth-day' periods in each cycle of time brings us exactly what we need, a driving and creative force to make it through to the next stage.

This next period is referred to as the 'fifth-night'. Historically these are periods of application or changing gear – that is when the discoveries of the fifth-day period are applied to life and if they don't work they will be changed or recycled! It's like a lull in the driving-force allowing things to settle before driving on again in the next day.

Consider that the discovery that mankind was using fire was followed by an Ice Age. Without the benefit of fire, man would have certainly perished. Evidence that Neanderthal man went extinct during the fifth-night period, after Homo Erectus had come to use art; could it be that because Neanderthal didn't have the capacity for creating art, is it possible that he could not create his future? Are these cycles showing us mere coincidence, or highlighting a repetitive cycle of evolution? Perhaps these are in patterns, like a fractal that we can see if we look carefully enough.

Art turning up during this fifth-day period promotes the idea that art is an advantage, and that it has a function in the evolving consciousness. Perhaps this is part of the reason – up there with speaking – why mankind succeeded in becoming the dominant species on this planet thus far. Could this mean in fact 'no art; no future', as Ian Xen Lungold suggests?

In conclusion, we can see that by using art, maths, science and shamanism in the form of this calendar to guide us, we can certainly interpret the cycles of time, helping us to understand what's been going on, what's happening now and also helping us predict what may happen in the future. If history does indeed repeat itself as the saying goes, and the calendar is bringing our attention to this new period, what may we expect next, in the lead up to 2012, the so called 'End Time'?

The arrival of the sixth-day on 12th November 2008 is predicted to bring in another Renaissance period according to this train of thought; a time of revival and re-birth. The last time this occurred was the 1960s, and look what happened then!

So following the premise that art has helped our species' success, I speculate further on its powerful attributes. This book, then, places major importance on Mandalas, the aspect of art that I consider to be one of the most accessible and universal tools for co-creation available to us today; and perhaps now it is time to reawaken it as widely as possible, during this current period of the sixth-day.

Is it synchronistic that we have recently been stirred up by Dan Brown's *DaVinci Code*, the explosion of Quantum Psychics, healings and psychic abilities at this particular time? Is the creative 'Geist' of Leonardo DaVinci, Jesus Christ, Albert Einstein, Carl Jung, Mozart and others being revived within us now? Could it be possible that their attributes have blended together in the field, which inspires each and every one of us alive today? Yes, yes and yes again...

So how will you face the opportunity of re-birthing your mind to use art, science and shamanism as a Mandala – a manifestation tool?

Still in denial, or ready to move into the light of awareness? I feel We do have the potential to tap into this knowledge available in the fields of energy in which we live, breathe and interact.

I get the sense we all must reactivate and apply our artistic skills straight away, and share this practice as widely as possible. We can co-create what we need; it's up to us to take responsibly and not pass off what happens as something beyond us.

We are the artisans, we are the scientists, and we are above all else the shamans of the 21st Century!

Chapter 8

I am That, I am... A Mandala

"Ehyeh asher ehyeh (I am that I am)"
~ Moses

Let's consider the idea introduced in Chapter 1, that each of us a living multi-sensory Mandala. We're not just separate organisms but containers for spirit; connective spirit that is whole and complete, however separate the facets may appear when confined within each body. As well as being containers for this omnipresent spirit, consider that we are containers for the essence and energy that we choose to take in from our environment outside.

It is therefore our responsibility to take in energy that makes our container healthy, and also to send out energy that makes our environment healthy. We are connected and symbiotic with the whole. We are fractals, putting meaning to chaos and evolving microcosms of the macrocosm.

As living multi-sensory Mandalas, we are capable of a certain amount of stability and transformation. These qualities, kept in balance, will allow us to be consistent, yet also to change as necessary. Being more aware of what affects our energy will benefit us, as well as everyone else, so each and every one of us is important to that end.

To be the best that we can be, from this perspective, is both our right and our responsibility. So what is the best that we can be, and how can we achieve it?

Understanding that we are a spirit within the body – the container for our essence, is a good place to begin. Awareness can be cultivated so that we take more notice of our own footprints, doubling our helpful qualities and halving our unhelpful ones.

We can learn how to keep our container connected and 'alive' with vibrant energy, and able to broadcast this beneficial energy into the collective energy-field. This is about understanding that whatever we take in the body and mind, will affect what we can, in turn, transmit out into the world.

Even things that seem random and chaotic have a system when we know how to see it. All is reflective, self-replicating and ultimately transformative.

When we get down to the basics, our personal appearance is the first part of our Mandala. The way we like to look, and how we dress, is an important part of our container. The messages we carry around on our body and about our person become part of our essence. The impact and energy of our appearance is not always apparent, yet it still has a powerful subconscious or even unconscious affect on everyone. Think of a single word that you believe any of your friends would use to describe you. Then go ahead and ask them. I am often aware of the mixed messages we give off and often wonder how conscious we are of what we are broadcasting. You will soon find out what you are broadcasting, based on what your friends tell you!

Our appearance changes the more aware we become. When you can look in the mirror and feel peaceful about what you see, instead of criticising, it is a sign you have achieved your natural form, whatever it is. You are seeing the true manifestation of your essence, its perfect container. You are able to shine and radiate the love you feel and the love you are being. We can all practise achieving this.

When I am in the gym getting changed after a workout, I often notice women moisturising their faces. I sometimes ask them, 'What are you thinking about now?' Once they get over the initial shock of someone asking such a thing, they often admit to being in the future, thinking about what they are going to do next –

perhaps shopping or going to work; rarely are they focused on their face. Yet they always seem delighted by my suggestion to focus on applying love or rejuvenation energy to their skin instead. This is a transformative self-loving practice, a simple and ongoing way to radiate loving thoughts to yourself and to others, through your face.

Our sound is another important aspect of our personal Mandala. Our voice changes tone. When you can listen to your own voice recorded and can feel good about it, rather than cringing, it is a sign that you have achieved your natural note, the truth of the essence that you contain. The more aware we become of our essence, the more comfortable we are taking responsibility for what we are. You are able to broadcast your essence through your voice, receive it through your body and be at peace with this sound aspect of divinity.

The energy of sound affects us whether we are aware of it or not. The way we speak, and the words we choose to use, are part of our ongoing sound Mandala.

I ask people on workshops to draw energy pictures of certain words, especially popular words that are used over and over, just to give us a powerful image of how the things we say could affect our aura. What we are sending out and what others are taking in. I have become more and more alert to the things that come out of my mouth now, and I have been actively training myself for several years to change my use of double negative in phrases such as 'not bad' in response to 'how are you?' using instead 'I'm good' or 'not so good', as the case may be. I feel so much better using the phrase 'yes I can', when asked to do something rather than saying 'no problem,' another double negative, which many people use today. Using negative words, whether by choice, or even through social conditioning and habit (which is very common), is a sure sign that you are focused on and attracting what you don't want.

If I ask someone how they are and they say 'not bad', I ask

them again to tell me how they are, instead of how they aren't! They look surprised, normally smile blankly at first and then after some silent thought, they get it, I see the penny drop as they tell me how they are! Next time, they may still reply with the habitual 'not bad', but then quickly change it as they realise what they did. Next time they pause to think before they reply to me. We are all the agents of change, and it's truly worth it!

The music we listen to also has an ongoing affect on us, and once again I am always looking to see how different sounds and music affects me personally, and how I notice the effects of it on others. I became aware of the noise of the extractor fan in my kitchen several years ago when I was cooking, then noticed the relief I suddenly felt as soon as I switched it off. A timely reminder of the power of sound!

The energy of the food we eat, how we eat it, as well as how we cook it, has a huge impact on us. You are what you eat, as the saying goes. I was reminded of this several years ago when I was cooking a meal while I was feeling upset. The meal looked good when I served it, but my close friends were able to tell me that it didn't taste up to my usual standard. My personal Mandala was broadcasting angst and they could taste it! Whatever we choose to eat becomes part of our personal Mandala, so if we do choose to eat meat, remember the energy of the kill is part of that intake.

When we stop mindlessly watching TV or doing other things as we eat, and pay attention to enjoying our meal, we will benefit enormously. As our awareness grows, our relationship with food changes. And as we change our relationship with food, our awareness grows even more. The cycle of conscious creation increases without effort once we begin. When we focus on food, it creates more energy and we naturally eat only what is appropriate; so we balance our system. We become exactly the right size, structure and form to suit our environment.

How we smell is also part of our personal Mandala. A clean and fresh-smelling body is a sign of self-love and respect. Looking after the body and even adorning it by applying fragrance carries a message to us through our physical body, and also to others in the air and space within us and around us. People can be very disturbed by unpleasant smells, and this disturbs the energy, which is not good for us or for the atmosphere around us. Stale smells and dirty clothing, smelling of cigarette , are a sign that we are unaware and uncaring. Attention to detail shows love and care.

How we are being is a fundamental part of our Mandala. Are we calm and serene, or are we excitable and noisy? Both cause a different energy and vibe at different times. When we sit down, do we position our body carefully and deliberately or do we just plonk ourselves down on the seat? Do we do a job carefully taking pride in it, or just get it done quickly without much care at all? Awareness affects all the ways in which we interact with our environment, which in turns affects the environment and ultimately how we feel, too.

The condition of our home and personal space is also a sign of loving and respecting our personal Mandala. We don't need a palace or mansion, but we do need to take care – to keep it clean and tidy, comfortable and practical.

Colour and décor hold energy, so be aware of these energies in your home. Your home affects you; it is symbiotic with you in that you rely on it and it on you. You need to care for it and alchemise its energy. It shelters and protects you so this is a two-way communication. Your home affects the quality of how you can relax and feel good. It takes some thought to begin with, but after a while good habits can be formed so that it becomes natural to be tidy and to take care. Be sure to create an atmosphere that feels nurturing and is nurtured. Next step is to spread that energy out slowly but surely into our street, community, town, city, county, country and planet – the jigsaw puzzle coming together piece by piece to complete the beautiful picture.

I had a wonderful opportunity to spread some lovely energy

in my community several months ago, and maybe even into the electricity grid nationally. My local electricity sub-station had blown up, and the engineers turned up to deal with it. Here's what happened:

I was about to drive to Salisbury to see my friend when unexpectedly I had a power cut. At first I ignored it, and carried on getting ready, but in a very short time I sensed that it was important and that I should take notice of what was happening. It lasted for maybe an hour, and then came back on. I left home, albeit a little later than planned, but in plenty of time for my appointment. However, by 3pm I received a phone call from my daughter telling me the engineers had come to dig up the local sub-station, and more than likely would have to dig up my driveway too. Also, they may need to leave vehicles on it, perhaps working all night. I asked her to have them call me if that had to happen so I could arrange access to my property later that night when I got home. At 5pm, Colin, the senior engineer called me from the site – he was very agitated. Somewhere along the line, the wires had got crossed, and he had the idea that I was refusing to give permission to use my drive. After clearing that up, he told me 6,000 people had been without power all day, and if he couldn't find the fault they would remain in the dark all night too. I wished him luck and said I'd be back later.

My friend and I did a meditation on this situation as she felt it was still significant and unresolved. During the meditation we were directed to put my Mandalas into the electricity supply so as to send positive energy through the electricity grid. I was astounded, but nevertheless agreed to do whatever I could if the power station was still open when I got home. It would be a lovely thing to do if it was possible to help in this way, and I looked forward to it.

On arrival home around 10pm that night, the whole neighbourhood was in darkness, the only lights coming from my house.

I thought it strange, but was grateful that my daughter had power and light. As I pulled into the drive Colin met me:

"You must be June."

"And you must be Colin."

We shook hands, and he apologised for the digging machine's making so much noise, but said it shouldn't last much longer. I offered to make tea, as we appeared to have power in the house. He could not explain how it was possible, and just said I was lucky! He then, unprompted, showed me inside the power station where they were digging, explaining all that had happened that day.

Well, I thought it was odd, but many odd things happen in my life, so I accepted it thinking I was supposed to see the big hole and all the pipes underground, so that I could visualise the Mandalas down there sending out their energy to the grid. Content in that plan, I left them to it and went home to bed! I meditated and visualised the Mandalas in the hole before drifting off into a contented sleep.

The doorbell rang at 7am and shook me from a deep slumber. I got up and pulled a fleece on top of my pyjamas to answer the door. A parcel delivery guy was on a mission to get his round finished by lunchtime, and most annoyed that there was no door number on my front wall. I was so surprised that I followed him out onto the road to see for myself, and sure enough someone had stolen my number! How odd, I thought, but it was all to become clear.

As synchronicity would have it, just then the electrical engineer walked into the drive and headed for the sub station – I would have missed him if the delivery guy hadn't brought me out to look for the number. So taking my courage into my hands, I ran after him and started to chat.

"Guess they found the fault last night then."

"Indeed they did, shortly after 10pm."

"Ah ha, shortly after I got home then, so what's happening

now?"

"I'm going to arrange to fill it in, probably this afternoon."

I took a deep breath and then, "Erm, I wonder if I could ask you a favour?"

" What sort of favour?" he frowned suspiciously, so I smiled, standing there in my slippers, Pj's and fleece with 'out of bed' hair!

"You might think this is a very strange request, but I've got these lovely stickers in the house and I would really like to put them on the electricity pipes underground so they can send healing energy out to the neighbourhood. I just thought it would be a lovely thing to do."

His face cracked into a half smile, and by now I figured he has to be thinking I am eccentric or mad or both.

"Go on then, get them," he humoured me.

"Great! Thanks, I won't be long."

By the time I got back down, he had opened up the sub-station and he was looking down into the hole. I went in and stood next to him looking down into the hole too. He looked at my slippers and pulled a face.

"You want me to do it don't you?"

"Well, that would be great, if you really don't mind."

No sooner said than done, he jumped down into the hole and looked up at me.

"Give 'em here then."

I pulled off the first sticker LOVE and passed it down to him. He looked at it and his body language changed instantly.

"Wow, that's nice." Then before I knew what had happened he seemed to be taken over.

" Right, give me the rest... We'll put Love on the incoming cable, this one, and then send out Peace and Joy to there and there, and Healing over here." He had it all planned out and then got out of the hole and stuck some on the station above ground too! I just watched him with a big smile on my face, and then as quickly as he tuned in, he came back to his senses and was suddenly embarrassed.

"Erm, we won't tell anybody about this will we? I'll just blame it on the kids if anyone asks me."

"Well, you may not want to tell anyone but you know what, I think it's amazing and I'm going to tell everyone. You're a star!"

He went off down the drive shaking his head in disbelief! I just had to laugh – oh and then tell everyone about the Power of Art!

As multi-sensory Mandalas ourselves, we can all be programmed by intent, and in this process we are moving into the realms of alchemy – as the previous story proves – where part of our consciousness is aware of other dimensions of reality and knowing, and can transform energy. As aware beings, we feel happier and more content, sure in the affects we have on others and confident in the energy we receive in return. We are indeed living containers for energy with the ability and responsibility to co-create our future as we interact with the omni-present quantum energy fields – divinity itself. I cannot explain encounters such as this in any other way.

This awareness can be conscious, subconscious on unconscious as we have seen, but once we make a decision to become more aware, to notice our effects more responsibly, we will be able to tune our personal Mandalas – the containers for our spirit – to reflect the qualities we choose, and in turn to affect others to become more aware. So if you are already mindful of your subtle energies, you will already know what you are capable of doing at a very deep level. Your Mandala currently contains the energy you brought in to it previously, yesterday and the day before. Tomorrow it will contain what you bring in today and tomorrow. Being aware of the energy you receive and broadcast is a huge step to becoming the best you can be. Our interaction with ourselves, with others and the planet, matters.

So if you are looking to benefit from this book, you will benefit. Remember that when two or more like minds come together, the energy magnifies. Maybe some of the true life-changing experiences shared will inspire some of your own. There is more than enough here to dip your toe in the water of what is possible, to share an understanding of co-creation and prayer, looking through the powerful lens of Art!

So to reiterate my main purpose, it is to re-introduce and remind everyone about the ultimate tool of manifestation and co-creation, the Mandala, and to re-establish it now during this powerful energy of the latest period of Renaissance, re-birth and revival, beginning in November 2008. And in doing so I am certain you will benefit from using this art – even if you still think you cannot draw!

Appendix 1

Contains references for further reading for those interested in a more detailed exploration of the ideas mentioned.

These scientists and parapsychologists are pushing the boundaries of what we believe may be possible as we explore Quantum Psychics and the nature of reality.

William Tiller PHD is currently Professor Emeritus of the Department of Materials Science and Engineering at Stanford University. During his work at Stanford he carried out experiments with Tibetan monks, and found that their intentions can 'condition' space on an atomic level. He is one of a few scientists to embrace this research unhindered by the scientific community's fearful and negative view of being able to reproduce these sorts of effects. He has pushed the boundary in order to make new discoveries and he is having very interesting results from his investigations.

In his latest book *'Psychoenergetic Science* ISBN-13: 978-1424338634', he states "My working hypothesis is that consciousness is a by-product, or emergent property, of spirit entering dense matter."

Jude Currivan PhD is a physicist, cosmologist, healer and mystic who has experienced multidimensional realities since early childhood. Her books offer a wonderful and empowering scientific vision of a world that is at last whole: *The Wave* (O Books) ISBN 1905047339 and *CosMos – a Co-creator's Guide to the Whole-World* (Hay House) ISBN 9781401918910 which is co-authored with philosopher and systems theorist Ervin Laszlo PhD. Weaving together the latest research across a wide range of fields they share the emerging perception of a meaningful and co-creative Cosmos that is exquisitely tuned to be 'as simple as it can be' for consciousness to explore itself.

Amit Goswami has been a professor of physics at the University of Oregon for 34 years. His new book *God Is Not Dead* ISBN-13: 978-1571745637 will change how readers think and experience the nature of reality, the existence of souls, the power of dreams, the universality of love, the possibility of ESP, and the very mind of God.

Bruce Lipton is a former medical school professor and research scientist. His experiments, and those of other leading-edge scientists, have examined in great detail the processes by which cells receive information. The implications of this research radically change our understanding of life and communication. *The Biology of Belief* ISBN-13: 978-0975991473 is a groundbreaking work in the field of New Biology. It shows that genes and DNA do not control our biology; instead DNA is controlled by signals from outside the cell, including the energetic messages emanating from our own positive and negative thoughts. Dr. Lipton's synthesis of the latest research in cell biology and quantum physics is being hailed as a major breakthrough showing that our bodies can be changed as we retrain our thinking.

William Tiller, in his book, *Some Science Adventures with Real Magic* ISBN-13: 978-1929331116 demonstrates how human intention can robustly affect physical properties from the pH of water to the maturation of fruit-fly larvae; also how this energy can be stored on electronic devices, and be reproduced at different locations and at other times. It explains how these results are attained based on quantum mechanics, thermodynamics, solid-state physics and electromagnetism.

Dean Radin, PhD, is Director of Research at the HESA Institute and Senior Fellow at the Institute of Noetic Sciences. In his book, *The Conscious Universe: The Scientific Truth of Psychic Phenomena* ISBN:0062515020 he has united the latest in high-tech experiments, including irrefutable data from his own groundbreaking research. With teachings of mystics and theories of quantum physics, Radin explores phenomena from ESP to ghosts and psychokinesis. Regarding psychic phenomena he states, "We know that these phenomena exist because of new ways of evaluating massive amounts of scientific evidence collected over a century by scores of researchers."

Appendix 2

Feedback from experiments instigated by June-Elleni Laine using Mandalas she created:

The first accounts share experiences of the Mandala for *PEACE*. Several examples are included here as they vary depending on how much the experimenter is influenced by their logical side and how much the ego tries to sabotage the interactions. This has been the most fascinating experiment so far. This Mandala helps to create a balanced cooperation between both sides of the brain. It means making time for awareness, which for many people is uncomfortable! But we can't have peace out there in the world until we have peace inside us. The mutual conflict inside our own brain is where we need to begin manifesting Peace, but will the left-brain cooperate?

This is what I wanted to find out. I noticed hostility and / or bewilderment from the left-brain reactions, as you will pick up in these accounts. Also, during workshops, I have noticed that those who attract this Mandala are often going through a very left-brain dominated phase in their lives… some think they simply don't need the Mandala, telling me they are already at peace. Even if they really believe this is true, the conversations I overhear about their lives tell a different story. The left-brain can be so manipulating!

I also find that people attract the Mandala when they are in a right-brain dominated phase when they cannot get to grips with the practicalities of life, they are always late for appointments and cannot organise themselves. Either way, the intention for Peace contained in this Mandala has evoked some interesting and sometimes uncomfortable interactions within people:

* * *

My first impression of the peace Mandala was that is was not an image that I would personally have chosen to look at. (Although I am not in the habit of contemplating Mandalas anyway) but just as a pleasing image to have around, I would not have chosen it. I realise that is because it is extremely stimulating to me. Interestingly, the relationship between the male/female in my own self has become a priority issue recently and have had unexpected help with this balance already. My first impression was that looking at this Mandala was like sucking lemons in my brain! It is disturbing and stimulating to me. I feel it is penetrating into a part of myself I don't know about. From lemons to laser beam. Mmmm yes, I am getting to feel some relationship to whatever it is this is about.

* * *

I wanted to ask you, because I am curious, did you create this Mandala purely instinctively, or did you think about the different elements. Of course I found myself analysing it and I have to say it is very, very clever.

* * *

After receiving it, I had an argument with an old friend over a long-standing problem. She is someone who exhibits a lot of traits that I personally find deplorable in women, which involves deep rivalry with other women, and control of men. I was very angry, and although the situation was not resolved (again) I was able to put it down and not try to force it to a resolution, but did not feel that I had capitulated in any way to something I do not support.

* * *

I am aware how much more necessary it is for the male and female, thinking and feeling sides to work together in the details of my own life.

And when this does happen, I can acknowledge it, and allow it to happen more, and to be able to swap from one to the other much more quickly, and even 'Yippee', let them work together simultaneously. I also remembered a dream again that I had when I was sixteen. I have occasionally done so throughout my life (I am 59). I dreamt that I was both male and female, and making love to myself. It's a dream I could have taken more notice of. Better late than never.

*   *   *

I have always had a tendency to live in the male side of myself. I like to think things through. I have not let myself trust my 'feelings' since I recognised a long time ago that they could be quite destructive both to myself, and other people. Of course, so can lack of feeling. But I always trusted logic!

Whilst meditating this week, for the first time ever I did not just calm down my over-energetic thinking machine, I found myself, rather than being aware of calming anxieties about money (lack of and other problems), instead flipping into a realisation of how rich and colourful my life is... deeper than that, my personal world, the actual colour in my life, the colours in my house, in my clothes, me, my personality and interests, my family, their personalities, their attention, their lives, born out of the darkness into the light. That is manifest. How deeply the opposites work together; thinking and feeling work together on a very deep level, deeper than I know.

Now, as I write this, the stimulation is travelling to my heart. I can feel the energy in my chest. It makes me want to laugh and cry.

*   *   *

Initial thoughts: I have found the peace Mandala quite difficult to look at. It was almost too bright, and the black was very uninviting for me. Although I felt that the black was very translucent – and not dark – there was something about it that I had to adjust to and with in order to be able to look at the Mandala properly. It then took on a softer energy – almost hazy – like a sunset seen over an ocean/sea.

* * *

I had the peace Mandala up on the background of my computer, and at first I spent a lot of time looking at it. Joining this experiment coincided with one of my monumental transformations / initiations. I found that when I was in the intense part of my journey I couldn't look at the Mandala anymore. I am not sure what role, if any, the Mandala played in speeding things up for me. At this point I am too afraid to look at it again – because it is all part of an old paradigm for me now. That is not to say the energy is old or tainted, but for me it served a purpose and I had to move on from it for now.

I have been in a rollercoaster and so many things have been provided to me to get me here, I feel sure that the Mandala was part of it too! I cannot yet describe what occurred for me as I am still in process, and am riding the wave of change and dealing with grief and pain as well as excitement and creation. Thinking of the Mandala makes my solar plexus fill with anxiety – where that anxiety comes from I am not totally sure, but it is part of my experience for now!

* * *

The HEALING Mandala seems to bring comfort, and is easily accepted by all who interact with it. In my experimenters' accounts here, and also feedback at workshops or after lectures, most people comment on the colour and some on the word:

* * *

The healing Mandala is beautiful, and my initial reaction was one of deep emotional response. My throat tightened, and tears came to my eyes. In my state of grief I find I do well until someone is really nice to me and asks about my husband. Then I have trouble controlling my emotions. My emotional reaction to seeing the Mandala was the same sort of reaction. The Mandala has light like I have seen and experienced in some of my best meditations. Even though it evoked tears, it was a good healing feeling.

* * *

Thank you for the healing Mandala. Colours have totally blown me away! Strangely, I am very drawn to these colours at present, and the word 'healing' is very much what I am currently going through. I will keep a journal, and forward it to you each month. I have used the Mandala as a wallpaper on my phone, so I have access to it throughout the day.

* * *

I have been very touched by the healing Mandala. My first reaction on seeing the Mandala continued for several days. I have laminated the Mandala, and have been setting my drinking water on it. I think I told you I have had the hardest nine months of my life. I have been dealing with the death of my Mother and husband of 51 years. It seems healing has come to me this week after a very low point the week before. I know that looking at the Mandala (especially with light behind it) gives me a feeling of being embraced, The rays of light seem to take the shape of loving arms or wings that give me a feeling of being powerfully loved. Thank you for bringing this into my life at just the right time.

* * *

It has been a healing month for me. My spirits are much better, and I have lost weight (have been trying since April to do so). The second and third week of the experiment I had all the symptoms of stomach flu. However it could have been part of what I need to do. That being to let go, to flush out the past and start anew. It does seem my healing started with the Mandala. I continue to use the Mandala as the opening page on my computer as well as other things, which you suggested. I will stay with it.

*   *   *

The Mandala for LIGHT was also acceptable to most people, and similar responses were reported. The intention for this Mandala was to clarify our light so that we know it's always there regardless of how things may appear. This doesn't represent sunlight, but the light feeling we have when in the sun or anywhere we think is sustaining and nurturing. The light feelings we have when we are connected to source or God. To increase our sense of what it is to be LIGHT to be connected, that we are light:

*   *   *

YES … the first comment was my reaction to the beautiful Mandala. I was overwhelmed by the light! It was strange that the blue is one of my favourite coloursI found the Mandala very calming and as I have been going through huge changes, I feel it has helped me to come to terms with those changes and has given me peace, as I have been very stressed. Part of it is that I believed it did, so not sure what part that plays in the process. . I looked at the Mandala most days especially before bed and I found that my dreaming was more active and more meaningful. Ritual is important. I looked at the Mandala and let it wash over me and sink into a deeper part of me and I believe it has helped with shifts I felt and still feel in myself.

*   *   *

It is a very powerful Mandala, and very universal and timeless, and thus I feel it can be used for many things, not just one request. The reference to light, made it easy for me to tune in to my guides more easily, and I have felt it easier to write things down and my poetry, more so than normal.

* * *

The LOVE Mandala creates the energy of unconditional love. It's not a pink heart, which to me represents ego love. The kind of love that is happy as long as the object of your love does what you want and gives you what you need. But that can turn to hate if this satisfaction is withdrawn! This Mandala creates a connection to love in a way we cannot understand, the love of SOURCE energy, the singularity. Bliss and divinity – the foundation of our very being that can never be disconnected, that continues after death and beyond.

* * *

The Love Mandala struck a lot of raw emotions; and emotions which have been dormant for many years have come to the surface for the first time, I feel like I want to acknowledge all the issues.... a feeling of emotional, physical de-cluttering. I know I have a long way to go, and I am sure I will have a few more wobbly emotional days.... but one step at a time.

* * *

I loved it – can't say how or why. Not what I had expected, but then I didn't know what to expect! I feel blessed.

* * *

ENLIGHTEN was created rather tongue in cheek. My intention was simply to put in the energy of lightening up and laughter with the potential to see past fear. I know we are all enlightened but for now we just forgot, so I imagine if and when we remember we would definitely smile! To achieve lightheartedness in Egyptian myth was essential for the onward journey to through the underworlds. They literally took out the heart of a corpse and weighed it and if it was too heavy you just didn't make it! Those who take their spiritual growth very seriously have issues with this Mandala. While others simply love it and are speechless at the simplicity. Hey, no one said enlightenment was a complicated thing, and as my Mother was born in Egypt, I decided to adopt the lighthearted way on this one!

* * *

It makes me laugh!

* * *

When I opened the Enlighten Mandala, printed it off and looked at it, its smile and eyes seemed to expand; they appeared to be getting bigger, and no, I hadn't been drinking! I now use the Mandala as my screen saver and have a laminated version on which I rest a glass of water before drinking it every day. It makes me smile, and the day begins I don't know if it is down to the Mandala or not, but I feel I am becoming more tolerant to those I wouldn't normally be, and I see more good in people and on the whole I am feeling more positive. I'm looking forward to carrying this experiment on and seeing what happens over the coming weeks.

* * *

About the Author

June-Elleni Laine is author of the book *The Art of Being ... Psychic – the power to free the artist within*

Its audio companion CD of the same name *is ideal for those who intend to develop their abilities another step beyond the limitations of the five senses. It features multidimensional sounds specifically created to resonate with subtle frequencies of the mind, body and soul. Used with exercises from the book, this audio companion guides you along the journey to develop extra sensory perception and heightened intuition, gaining validation of psychic abilities that surpass the self-imposed limitations of logical thinking.*

Her website is http://www.psychicartworks.com/

Workshops and Retreats

Initiating The Power To Create through Psychic Art

This work teaches how to develop psychic ability and increase creative potential utilising the arts in an enjoyable way. I promote this ability as a natural human development, rather than a mystical phenomenon attained exclusively by the 'chosen few'. How can developing psychic ability help us all? By developing our true potential, we intuitively become more aware of our actions, and the consequences of those actions. We can choose to add responsible thoughts to the mass consciousness and create a more positive future.

By exploring right-brain and left-brain aptitude, we are better able to experience and understand the relationship between our logical self and our intuitive self, so learning how to balance them in a more helpful way. Understanding the conflict that can often occur within our own thoughts is vital in using this ability efficiently. By seeing this conflict within, often sheds light on why we witness conflict out there!

This will, without doubt, help us to move towards achieving a better state of health and balanced well-being for the entire planet. Every single person has their part to play, whatever we do affects the whole. Everyone counts!

Private Readings

Private readings are available in person in London and Surrey, as well as by telephone, email or online instant messenger. *For telephone or Internet readings art- work will be sent out by post or email as preferred. A recording of a telephone reading or reading in person can be made onto CD.*

Spirit Portraits Readings

A reading consists of one or more portraits of spirit in a session depending upon the amount of clairvoyant information received. You can request a loved one, or a spiritual guide to come through. Connections to loved ones can help with the grieving process, while connecting to a spirit guide helps many people along their own life journey, advising on current issues they may have. I have no control over which particular spirit comes through, I simply place an intention and the rest is left to spirit. Because of free will in this world and the next, we cannot be sure if the loved one in your thoughts will be the one who shows up, although it is often the case that they do. It is important to realise this before embarking on a reading. Each reading is different, and an exciting experiment in its own right.

Clients are frequently surprised by the energy of the portraits produced when I connect with the energy of the spirit communicator. Even without a logical explanation for this phenomenon, many clients feel encouraged by the connection and an emotional healing often takes place, leading them to further their own spiritual path in life. Other clients, however, can be a little shocked by this experience of something seemingly beyond the physical dimension. They can choose apprehension and / or denial, mostly because the comfort of their belief structure has been challenged.

A Mandala Consultation

This private session consists of advice on purpose and making a Mandala. During this session you will set your intentions and co-create a Mandala designed for your individual needs. The power of Mandalas is a tool for manifestation of intention. It is not just about creating art, it's about creating your life.

Using Clearing, Healing and Self-Enquiry Mandalas, I have witnessed clients clear energy blocks caused by various life issues, phobias, help those who have low self esteem or who are creatively blocked. Manifestation Mandalas have helped people to attract assets from increased creativity to a lovely new home! Healing Mandalas are self explanatory and are very powerful aids to physical and mental well being.

June-Elleni Laine at The College Of Psychic Studies
16, Queensberry Place, South Kensington, London SW7 2EB, United Kingdom.

To book a reading in person at the College in London call
+44 (0)20 7589 3292
Voice Mail: +44(0) 208 395 2140
Email: info@psychicartworks.com

Notes

Introduction

Different strands of science and the media are exploring ideas that could change how many of us view life, the universe and everything.

1 Journalist and Spiritual seeker Lynne McTaggart's best selling book The Intention Experiment ISBN 978-0007194582 blends elements of quantum physics with stories of ordinary people with extraordinary experiences and tales of scientists from some of the most prestigious universities in the world researching into the areas of psychic phenomena and the power of human thought.

Chapter 1

coming to light mostly through ... hypnosis, art therapy and more recently NLP.

2 NLP – Neuro Linguistic Programming is a form of mental mapping, made popular by Robert Dilts, John Grinder and Roger Bandler (1980), the co-founders of the discipline. It can often interpret the subconscious messages into the conscious mind.

Modern day anthropologists, such as Marianne George, who lived amongst the Barok tribe in Papua New Guinea, reportedly experienced the amazing capacity of dreams

3 Ref Paul Devereux- Moveable Feast from Mind Before Matter ISBN 9781846940576

eventually I overcame my initial anxieties – including several unexplainable experiences

4 Details of these experiences can be found in my book The Art Of Being... Psychic ISBN 1905047541

You can watch the neuro-anatomist Dr Jill Bolte-Taylor's video
5   The video is available on line at
http://blog.ted.com/2008/03/jill_bolte_tayl.php#more and her
book *My Stroke Of Insight* (ISBN 978-1430300618) is a detailed
account of her timely experience.

Nobel Prize winner Dr Roger Woolcote Sperry
6   In1981 Nobel Prize winner, Roger Wolcott Sperry, showed that
the left and right hemispheres of the brain were able to
function independently and had different areas of expertise.
The left side normally used for logic and objective thought
patterns such as language, while the right hemisphere previously thought of as the mute 'sleeping' partner, used for
creative and subjective tasks, such as music and spatial
awareness. His work showed that by severing the corpus
callosum – the connection between the brain hemispheres –
both hemispheres could be shown to operate independently. In
an article at Nobelprize.org Norman H. Horrowitz writes *"By
devising ways of communicating with the right hemisphere, Sperry
could show that this hemisphere is, to quote him: "indeed a conscious
system in its own right, perceiving, thinking, remembering,
reasoning, willing, and emoting, all at a characteristically human
level, and . . . both the left and the right hemisphere may be conscious
simultaneously in different, even in mutually conflicting, mental
experiences that run along in parallel."*

Chapter 2
Vaastu or Feng Shui placement
7   Vaastu is the ancient Indian art of placement and Feng Shui is
an offshoot. See Mystic Living ISBN 1905047983 by Raymond
Prohs for more information.

the Japanese scientist Dr Masuro Emoto is doing experiments on
water

8   Dr Masuro Emoto appeared in the Movie What The Bleep Do
     We Know, which open the doors for many to discover more
     about the energy of intent and creation. He shows that by
     simply adding a label that says 'love' or 'thank you' onto the
     bottle of water and then freezing it, Dr Emoto finds the
     crystals formed in the frozen water are more balanced,
     detailed and visually pleasing than water that has been
     labelled with negative words, which forms deformed crystals.
     Although science argues there isn't a standard by which to test
     this process scientifically, and this is quite true because every
     natural crystal is unique and therefore the same results cannot
     be reproduced exactly. However what they fail to
     acknowledge is that the crystals do show change. It is this
     'change' that indicates 'something' has happened to the water!

Rupert Sheldrake reports on this work in his book
9   Dr Rupert Sheldrake's book The Sense of Being Stared At (ISBN
     009179643)

the 'Joy' Mandala
10   If you are interested to explore the complete set of Mandalas,
     please refer to my website on www.psychicartworks.com and
     to read more interesting feedback I received on reactions to the
     other Mandalas in the range, see Appendix 2.

Chapter 3
the 'Law of Two or More'
11   "If two of you on earth agree about anything you ask for, it will be
     done for you by my Father in heaven. For where two or three come
     together in my name, there am I with them" (Matthew 18:19-20).

I use the ancient art of Ayurveda for my guidance
12   Ayur means Life, Veda means science, Ayurveda is an ancient Indian
     system of understanding life and health, it stems back over 3,000

years and was intuited by seers.

the principles of Ayurveda for timing
13 *For more reading on the many aspects of Ayurveda, I recommend books by Robert Svoboda or David Frawley. For Ayurvedic timing called Panchang see Michael Geary.*

sound ceremonies in workshops
14 You can experience this for yourself by attending a Mandala-making workshop, details of which are on my website events page, but you could also get an idea of it by listening to Tracks 6 and 7 on the companion CD to *The Art Of Being ... Psychic*. This CD contains powerful sound Mandalas specifically to trigger the intuitive right-side of the brain.

blessing and thanks to food before you eat it, adds positive energy
15 I'd like to recommend *Cooking With Love* by Wendy Horne, designed for sensitive beings, delicious and wholesome vegetarian, gluten free and dairy free recipe book.

residual energy
16 The energy left in a building or structure by activities that were conducted in that place. Can be the energy of someone who lived there or even the energy of a violent act committed there. Holy places too have residual energy due to constant praying or communion with God.

Chapter 4
ground yourself back into your normal awareness afterwards
17 A video is available on my website www.psychiart works.com in multi-media, and it is also freely-available on youtube.com (search June-Elleni Laine) which shows an effective cleansing technique and for closing the chakras.

the 90-second rule

[18] Thoughts that spontaneously come into our mind, both good and not so good, only last about 60 to 90 seconds naturally; anything longer than that means we have consciously decided to keep thinking about it. Good one to try when you react, rather than respond to something – count to 90 before responding and see how you deal with it then.

come along and do a workshop or retreat with me

[19] If you prefer individual attention have a Mandala experience in person, or by phone. More information can be found on my website www.psychicartworks.com/readings.html

Chapter 7

the ancient Mayan calendar

[20] The Mayan Calendar is thought to be a record of the evolving consciousness or creative principle. The periods of time mapped on the calendar are divided up into 7 days and 6 nights – 13 periods – Each one of these days and nights lasts for one thirteenth of a cycle of time. The calendar is shaped like a pyramid, depicting 9 cycles of time or steps, each one becoming shorter the closer it gets the top. Each day and night has its own schedule, whereby it evokes particular creative principles to reoccur each cycle on the same day or night. So if the cycle was 16.4 billion years long, at the bottom step of the pyramid, each day would last 1.26 billion years; quite a long time to apply its creative principle. Higher up the pyramid when a cycle is 256 years each day would be 19.7 years and so on. Giving us a sense of time speeding up. Today each one of these 13 periods is only 360 days, so in effect we are now creating in about a year, what took about 20 years when I was a child. No wonder we feel everything and everyone is moving faster! For more information on this interpretation see Dr Carl Calleman's book *The Mayan Calendar* ISBN:0970755805

BOOKS

O is a symbol of the world, of oneness and unity. In different cultures it also means the "eye," symbolizing knowledge and insight. We aim to publish books that are accessible, constructive and that challenge accepted opinion, both that of academia and the "moral majority."

Our books are available in all good English language bookstores worldwide. If you don't see the book on the shelves ask the bookstore to order it for you, quoting the ISBN number and title. Alternatively you can order online (all major online retail sites carry our titles) or contact the distributor in the relevant country, listed on the copyright page.

See our website **www.o-books.net** for a full list of over 500 titles, growing by 100 a year.

And tune in to myspiritradio.com for our book review radio show, hosted by June-Elleni Laine, where you can listen to the authors discussing their books.

MySpiritRadio